Kickstart C Programming Fundamentals

Learn C Programming Basics, Pointers, Data Structures, Memory Management, and File Handling with Hands-On Examples and Practice Exercises

Dr. Dipra Mitra

www.orangeava.com

First Published: May 2026

Published By: Orange Education Pvt Ltd, AVA®

Address: 9, Daryaganj, Delhi, 110002, India

275 New North Road Islington Suite 1314 London,
N1 7AA, United Kingdom

ISBN (PBK): 978-93-49887-63-3
ISBN (E-BOOK): 978-93-49887-23-7

Scan the QR code to explore our entire catalogue

www.orangeava.com

Get a Free eBook

We hope you're enjoying your recent book purchase! Your feedback is incredibly valuable to us and helps other readers discover books that truly make a difference.

If you found this book useful or enjoyable, we'd greatly appreciate it if you could leave a short review with a 5-star rating on Amazon. Your review supports our work and allows us to reach more learners worldwide.

As a thank-you, we're happy to offer you a **free digital copy of this book** plus a **30% discount code** for your next purchase on our official websites:

www.orangeava.com

www.orangeava.in (For the Indian Subcontinent).

☑ **How it works:**

Leave your review on Amazon, take a screenshot of the confirmation or use the following link to submit the claim and email it to **info@orangeava.com.** Once received the required detail, we will send your rewards within 24 hours, **along with one month free subcription to the book on AVA SkillShelf!**

Claim Form

https://rebrand.ly/4d2477

Thank you for your support—it truly means a lot to us.

Downloading the code bundles and colored images

Please follow the links or scan the QR codes to download the
Code Bundles and Images of the book:

https://github.com/ava-orange-education/Kickstart-C-Programming-Fundamentals

The code bundles and images of the book are also hosted on
https://rebrand.ly/9zy4e59

In case there's an update to the code, it will be updated on the existing GitHub repository.

Errata

We take immense pride in our work at **Orange Education Pvt Ltd,** and follow the best practices to ensure the accuracy of our content to provide an indulging reading experience to our subscribers. Our readers are our mirrors, and we use their inputs to reflect and improve upon human errors, if any, that may have occurred during the publishing processes involved. To let us maintain the quality and help us reach out to any readers who might be having difficulties due to any unforeseen errors, please write to us at:

errata@orangeava.com

Your support, suggestions, and feedback are highly appreciated.

Dedicated to

My Beloved Parents:

Shri Prasanta Mitra,
Shreemati Dipti Mitra.

And

My Wife, Madhuchhanda Mitra,
My Son, Diptendu Kumar Mitra.

About the Author

Dr. Dipra Mitra is an academician, researcher, and educator in the field of Computer Science and Engineering. He is deeply committed to teaching, research, and the advancement of computing technologies. His academic interests include programming, artificial intelligence, machine learning, data science, and smart agricultural technologies, with a focus on connecting theoretical knowledge with practical applications.

Dr. Mitra has contributed to several research publications in reputed journals and conferences. His research primarily focuses on developing intelligent systems that address real-world challenges, particularly in agriculture and sustainable technology. He has worked on projects related to plant disease detection, smart farming solutions, and AI-based decision-support systems that assist farmers in improving crop productivity and management practices. Through these initiatives, he aims to apply modern technological tools to solve practical societal problems.

Alongside his research work, Dr. Mitra has extensive experience teaching core computer science subjects, including programming, data structures, and emerging technologies. He strongly believes in a practical, student-centered approach to learning that encourages logical thinking, creativity, and strong problem-solving skills. Over the years, he has mentored many students and inspired them to explore research-oriented learning and innovation.

Dr. Mitra is also actively involved in developing educational resources and academic materials designed to make technical subjects more accessible to beginners. His motivation for writing this book stems from a desire to help students build a solid foundation in programming and computational thinking.

Beyond his professional activities, Dr. Mitra enjoys reading, exploring emerging technological trends, and participating in academic collaborations that promote knowledge sharing and innovation.

About the Technical Reviewer

Sarthak Shah is a Senior Software Engineer and Technical Lead with over a decade of experience designing high-performance, large-scale distributed systems and real-time decision platforms. His work focuses on building low-latency, fault-tolerant infrastructure that powers critical decision-making systems at scale, with deep expertise in systems engineering, cloud-native architectures, and performance-critical programming, including C++.

He has contributed to complex engineering systems across leading technology organizations such as Microsoft, Intel, and Amazon, where his work has centered on designing and scaling backend infrastructure that operates under stringent latency and reliability constraints. At Amazon Ads, he leads the development of real-time evaluation and decisioning systems that process high-volume traffic and enable efficient, data-driven outcomes in production environments.

Sarthak's technical interests lie at the intersection of distributed systems, intelligent automation, and agentic architectures, with a focus on integrating AI into production-grade systems without compromising reliability or performance. He is an active contributor to the broader engineering community through technical reviews and knowledge-sharing initiatives.

He is passionate about building systems that combine rigorous engineering principles with practical scalability, and his work continues to advance the design of resilient, high-throughput platforms for real-world applications.

Acknowledgments

I would like to express my sincere gratitude to everyone who supported and encouraged me during the writing of this book. First and foremost, I am deeply thankful to my parents for their constant motivation, encouragement, and belief in me. Their unwavering support has been a great source of strength throughout this journey of mine.

I am also grateful to the institutions, courses, and organizations that have contributed immensely to my learning and development as well as the successful completion of this book. The knowledge and resources they provided helped me strengthen my understanding of programming concepts, and inspired me to share this knowledge through this book.

My special thanks goes to Mr. Sourabh Dwivedi and his team at Orange Education Pvt. Ltd. for their valuable technical insights and thoughtful suggestions during the preparation of this book. I would also like to thank my colleagues and well-wishers for their encouragement and support, which allowed me the time and motivation needed to complete this work successfully.

Preface

Programming has become one of the most essential skills in today's technology-driven world. Among the many programming languages available, C programming holds a special place as one of the most fundamental and widely used languages. It serves as the foundation for understanding advanced programming concepts, and helps learners build strong logical and problem-solving skills. This book has been written with the objective of providing a clear and structured introduction to the fundamentals of C programming.

The content of this book is designed to guide beginners' step by step through the vital concepts of programming. Starting with the basics of computer systems and program structure, the book gradually introduces important topics such as operators, control statements, arrays, algorithms, functions, recursion, pointers, structures, and file handling. Each chapter is explained in a simple and practical manner with examples and programs that help readers understand how theoretical concepts are applied in real programming scenarios.

This book is intended primarily for students, beginners, and anyone interested in learning programming using C. The goal is to help readers develop a strong foundation in programming concepts and logical thinking. Additionally, by practicing the examples and exercises provided in the book, readers will gain the confidence to write their own programs, and explore more advanced areas of computer science and software development.

Chapter 1: This chapter will cover the basics of programming, evolution of languages, structure of C program, computer system components, compiler, and interpreter.

Chapter 2: It will cover constants, variables, data types, arithmetic operators, logical operators, precedence, and associativity.

Chapter 3: This will cover the fundamental concepts of decision making and looping in C programming, which help control the flow of a program. Decision-making statements allow programs to execute different actions based on conditions, while looping statements enable repeated execution of a set of instructions.

The chapter will also cover important decision-making constructs such as if statements, if-else statements, nested if statements, and switch statements. These statements help programmers implement logical conditions, and control how programs respond to different inputs and situations.

Chapter 4: This chapter will cover the concept of arrays in C programming, which allow programmers to store multiple values of the same data type in a single variable. Arrays help organize data efficiently, and make it easier to process large amounts of information using a single structure.

The chapter will also cover one-dimensional and two-dimensional arrays, explaining how data can be stored and accessed in linear and tabular forms. Readers will learn how arrays are declared, how elements are accessed using index positions, and how arrays are used in various programming tasks.

Chapter 5: This chapter will cover the basic concept of algorithms and their importance in problem solving as well as programming. An algorithm is a step-by-step procedure used to solve a problem or perform a specific task efficiently. Understanding algorithms helps programmers design clear and logical solutions before implementing them in codes.

Chapter 6: This chapter will cover the concept of functions in C programming, which help in dividing a large program into smaller and manageable parts. Functions improve program readability, reusability, and maintainability by allowing programmers to organize codes into logical blocks.

This chapter will also cover function declaration and function definition, explaining how functions are created and used within a program. It will also discuss arguments and return values, which enable functions to receive input data and return results to the calling program.

Chapter 7: This explains the concept of recursion in C programming, where a function calls itself to solve a problem. Recursion is a powerful technique used to break complex problems into smaller and simpler subproblems, making them easier to solve.

The chapter will cover recursive functions and their structure, explaining how a recursive call works, and the importance of a base condition to stop the recursion. Understanding this concept helps programmers design efficient solutions for problems that follow repetitive patterns.

Chapter 8: It explains the concept of structures in C programming, which allows programmers to group different types of data under a single name. Structures are useful for representing complex data such as records containing multiple related attributes.

Chapter 9: This chapter will cover the basic concept of pointers in C programming. Pointers are variables that store the memory address of another variable, allowing programmers to work directly with memory, and manage data efficiently.

The chapter will also cover pointer declaration, initialization, and pointer arithmetic, explaining how pointers can be used to access and manipulate data stored in memory. It will also discuss pointers with arrays and pointers with functions, demonstrating how pointers help in efficient data handling, and passing data between functions.

Chapter 10: This explains the fundamental concepts of file handling in C, which enable programs to store data permanently, and retrieve it whenever required. File handling is important when working with large amounts of data that need to be saved beyond program execution.

DID YOU KNOW

Did you know that Orange Education Pvt Ltd offers eBook versions of every book published, with PDF and ePub files available? You can upgrade to the eBook version at **www.orangeava.com** and as a print book customer, you are entitled to a discount on the eBook copy. Get in touch with us at: **info@orangeava.com** for more details.

At **www.orangeava.com**, you can also read a collection of free technical articles, sign up for a range of free newsletters, and receive exclusive discounts and offers on Print Books and eBooks.

PIRACY

If you come across any illegal copies of our works in any form on the internet, we would be grateful if you would provide us with the location address or website name. Please contact us at **info@orangeava.com** with a link to the material.

ARE YOU INTERESTED IN AUTHORING WITH US?

If there is a topic that you have expertise in, and you are interested in either writing or contributing to a book, please write to us at **business@orangeava.com**. We are on a journey to help developers and tech professionals to gain insights on the present technological advancements and innovations happening across the globe and build a community that believes Knowledge is best acquired by sharing and learning with others. Please reach out to us to learn what our audience demands and how you can be part of this educational reform. We also welcome ideas from tech experts and help them build learning and development content for their domains.

REVIEWS

Please leave a review. Once you have read and used this book, why not leave a review on the site that you purchased it from? Potential readers can then see and use your unbiased opinion to make purchase decisions. We at Orange Education would love to know what you think about our products, and our authors can learn from your feedback. Thank you!

For more information about Orange Education, please visit **www.orangeava.com**.

Table of Contents

1. **Introduction to C Programming** 1
Introduction 1
Structure 1
Why Learn C 2
Basic Features of C 2
Introduction to Components of a Computer System 3
Operating System 7
Batch Operating System 8
Time-Sharing (Multitasking) Operating System 8
Distributed Operating System 9
Network Operating System 9
Real-Time Operating System 9
Mobile Operating System 9
Embedded Operating System 10
Multi-User and Single-User Operating Systems 10
Multiprocessing Operating System 10
Compilers 11
Interpreter 11
Assembler 11
Algorithm 11
Example of Algorithm: Find the Largest of Three Numbers 12
Conclusion 15
Exercises 16

2. **Arithmetic Expressions and Precedence** 17
Introduction 17
Structure 17
Identifiers 18
Types 18
Constants 20

Symbolic Constants ... 21

`printf` Conversion Specifiers ... 22

Declarations ... 22

Arithmetic Operations ... 23

Relational and Logical Operations ... 25

Bitwise Operators ... 27

Type Conversions and Casts ... 28

Conclusion ... 30

Exercises ... 30

3. Branching and Iteration ... 32

Introduction ... 32

Structure ... 32

Branching ... 33

Conclusion ... 44

Exercises ... 44

4. Arrays ... 46

Introduction ... 46

Structure ... 46

Introduction to Arrays ... 47

One-Dimensional Array (1-D Array) ... 48

Two-Dimensional Array (2-D Array) ... 49

Multi-Dimensional Array (M-D Array) ... 52

Array Traversal ... 53

Array of Pointers ... 56

Pointer to an Array ... 57

Conclusion ... 58

Questions ... 59

5. Algorithms ... 60

Introduction ... 60

Structure ... 60

Characteristics of a Good Algorithm ... 60

Representations of Algorithms 61
Classification of Algorithms 62
Common Algorithms with Examples 62
Searching Algorithms 62
Linear Search 63
Binary Search 63
Sorting Algorithms 65
Bubble Sort 65
Complexity 66
Asymptotic Notation 67
Big-O Notation (O) 68
Omega Notation (Ω) 68
Theta notation(Θ) 69
Conclusion 71
Questions 71

6. C Function 73
Introduction 73
Structure 73
Types of Functions 73
Library Functions 74
User-Defined Functions 74
Formal Parameters and Actual Parameters 75
Passing Parameters to Functions or Types of Argument Passing 78
Call by Value 78
Call by Address 79
Storage Classes 81
Global Variables 81
Local Variables (Automatic Variables) 82
Static Variables 82
Register Variables 83
Program 1: A Given Number is an Armstrong Number or Not Using a Function 83

Program 2: A Given Number is a Palindrome or Not Using a Function 84
Conclusion 85
Multiple Choice Questions 85
Questions 86

7. C Recursion 88
Introduction 88
Structure 88
Stack Frame Explanation 88
Types of Functions 89
Direct Recursion 89
Indirect Recursion 90
Tail Recursion 91
No Tail/Head Recursion 91
Head Recursion 91
Quicksort Using Recursion 93
Complexity Analysis of QuickSort 94
Merge Sort Using Recursion 95
Power of a Number Using Recursion 96
Conclusion 98
Exercises 98

8. Structures and Unions 99
Introduction 99
Structure 99
Defining and Declaring Structures 100
Declaration and Syntax 100
Creating Structure Variables 101
Initialization of Structures 102
Initialization and Accessing Structure Members 102
The Dot Operator (.) 102
Sample Program: Structure Input and Output 103
Memory Layout and Structure Padding 104

- *Contiguous Storage* 104
- *Structure Padding* 105
- *Sample Program: Verifying Padding* 106
- *Structure Assignment (Copying)* 106
- *Sample Program: Structure Copy* 107

Array of Structures 108
- *Definition* 108
- *Accessing Array Elements* 108
- *Sample Program: Creating a Student Database* 109

Pointers to Structures 111
- *Definition* 111
- *Sample Program: Pointer to Structure* 111

Nested Structures 113
- *Accessing Nested Members* 114
- *Sample Program: Nested Structures* 114

Passing Structures to Functions 115
- *Pass by Value* 115
- *Pass by Reference (Using Pointers)* 116
- *Sample Program: Passing Structures* 116

Unions and their Memory Management 117
- *Definition* 117
- *Memory Allocation in Unions* 118
- *Accessing Union Members* 118
- *Sample Program: Union Behavior* 118

Conclusion 120

Questions 120

Programming Exercises 121

9. Pointers 122

Introduction 122

Structure 122

Definition and Concepts 123

Declaration of Pointers 123

Core Operators: & and * 124
Sample Program: Basic Pointer Usage 124
Why Typed Pointers (int* versus float*) 125
Pointer Arithmetic 126
The Rule of Scaling 126
Valid Operations 127
Pointers and Arrays 127
The Array Name as a Pointer 128
Accessing Array Elements 128
Sample Program: Traversing an Array Using Pointers 128
Functions and Pointers: Call by Reference 129
The Problem with Call by Value 129
The Solution: Call by Reference 130
Pointer to Pointer (Double Pointers) 131
Generic Pointers (void *) 131
NULL Pointers 132
Dangling Pointers 132
Returning the Address of a Local Variable 132
Pointer to Freed Memory 133
Wild (Uninitialized) Pointers 133
Const Correctness with Pointers 133
`sizeof` Pitfalls: `sizeof(ptr)` vs `sizeof(*ptr)` 134
NULL vs 0 in C 134
Conclusion 135
Questions 135
Programming Exercises 135

10. File Handling and String Handling in C 136
Introduction 136
Structure 136
Definition and Concepts 137
Types of Files 137
The `FILE` Pointer 137

Opening a File (`fopen`) 138
Closing a File (fclose) 138
Sample Program: Creating and Opening a File 139
Reading and Writing Text Files 140
Character I/O (`fputc` and `fgetc`) 140
String I/O (`fputs` and `fgets`) 140
Formatted I/O (`fprintf` and `fscanf`) 141
Sample Program 1: Writing to a File 141
Sample Program 2: Reading from a File 142
Reading and Writing Binary Files 143
Writing Binary Data: `fwrite()` 144
Reading Binary Data: `fread()` 144
Sample Program: Writing Structures to a Binary File 144
Sample Program: Reading Structures from a BinaryFile 145
Random Access in Files 147
rewind() 147
ftell() 147
fseek() 147
Sample Program: Random Access 148
Error Handling in File Operations 149
String Handling 150
Declaration and Initialization of Strings 150
Input and Output of Strings 150
`scanf()` Function 151
`gets()` Function (Unsafe / Deprecated) 151
`puts()` Function 152
C Program Using Common String Functions 153
Conclusion 156
Questions 156
Programming Exercises 157

Index 158

CHAPTER 1

Introduction to C Programming

Introduction

The history of C programming can be traced back to the 1960s, when computer scientists began exploring high-level languages for system development. One such language was **Basic Combined Programming Language (BCPL)**, developed by **Martin Richards** in the year 1966. It was a typeless language designed mainly for writing system software. This inspired the creation of a simpler language called **B**, developed by **Ken Thompson** at Bell Labs in 1969, which was used primarily for early versions of the Unix Operating System. However, B had limitations, especially in terms of data handling and type structures. To overcome the limitations of B, **Dennis Ritchie** at Bell Labs developed the **C programming language** in the year **1972**. C retained the simplicity of B, but introduced powerful features like data types, structured programming constructs (such as loops and conditionals), and pointer-based memory access. This made C a much more flexible and an efficient tool for system-level programming, specifically for writing operating systems.

Today, C continues to play a pivotal role in software development. It is widely used in operating systems, embedded systems, compilers, device drivers, and performance-critical applications. Many modern programming languages such as C++, Java, and Python have been influenced by C. Its efficiency and close-to-hardware capabilities make it an essential language for understanding computer systems and low-level programming.

Structure

In this chapter, we will cover the following topics:

- Basic Concept of C Programming
- Structure of the C Program
- Basic Concept of the Operating System and Its Type

- Introduction to Components of a Computer System
- Operating System

Why Learn C

Foundational Language: Many modern languages including C++, Java, and Python are influenced by C.

- **High Performance**: C allows direct access to memory and hardware, making it suitable for system-level programming.
- **Portability**: C programs can run on many different types of systems with little or no modification.
- **Understanding of Computer Fundamentals**: Learning C helps you understand how computers work at a lower level, such as memory management and data storage.

Basic Features of C

Structured Language: It organizes code using functions and control structures.

- **Rich Set of Operators**: Supports arithmetic, logical, relational, and bitwise operations.
- **Modularity**: Code can be broken into functions for better readability and maintenance.
- **Efficient**: Programs written in C are fast, and uses system resources quite effectively.

Structure of a Simple C Program

```
#include <stdio.h>
        int main()
           {
printf("Hello, World!\n");
                  return 0;
           }
```

The preceding code encompasses:

- **Preprocessing:** The directive #include is substituted with the contents of **`stdio.h`**.
- **Compilation**: The code is converted into assembly instructions for x86 or x86_64 architectures.
- **Assembly:** Assembly is transformed into object code (**`.obj`** file).

- **Linking**: Establishes connections with the C runtime (for example, `msvcrt.dll`). Generates a Windows PE (Portable Executable) file. greetings.exe.

Key Concepts Introduced:

- **Syntax and Semantics**: Understanding how to write correct C code.
- **Data Types and Variables**: Declaring and using variables of different types.
- **Input and Output**: Using `scanf ()` and `printf ()` for user interaction.
- **Control Structures:** Using conditions and loops to control program flow.
- **Functions:** Breaking code into reusable blocks.

Before learning the C programming language in depth, it is important to understand the basic components of a computer system. Since C interacts closely with hardware and system resources, having a clear understanding of how a computer works will help learners better grasp programming concepts.

Introduction to Components of a Computer System

A computer system is a combination of hardware and software that work together to perform tasks and process data. Understanding the key components of a computer system is essential for anyone beginning their journey in computer science or information technology.

- **Input Unit:** The input unit comprises of devices connected to the computer for data entry. These devices receive input and translate it into a binary code which is comprehensible to the computer. Common input devices include the keyboard, mouse, joystick, and scanner. The Input Unit consists of one or more input devices connected to a computer. A user provides data and commands using input devices, including a keyboard and mouse. The input unit supplies data to the processor for subsequent processing.
- **Central Processing Unit:** The Central Processing Unit (CPU) serves as the computer's brain, governing all its operations. Upon inputting data via an input device, the CPU processes the information. Initially, it retrieves instructions from memory, subsequently decoding them to comprehend the required actions. It pulls data from the memory or an input device when necessary. Subsequently, the CPU does the work and either retains the result or presents it on an output device. The CPU comprises of three primary components: the Arithmetic Logic Unit (ALU), responsible for computations and logical operations; the Control Unit (CU).
- **Arithmetic and Logic Unit (ALU):** The ALU performs arithmetic and logical operations. Arithmetic operations include addition, subtraction, multiplication,

and division. Logical operations involve comparing data values to determine relationships such as greater than, less than, or equal to. The ALU is a key component of the CPU and is responsible for carrying out calculations required by programs.

- **Control Unit:** The Control Unit orchestrates and regulates the data flow to and from the CPU, while also managing the activities of the ALU, memory registers, and input/output units. It is also tasked with executing all the commands stored in the program. The system decodes the retrieved instruction, interprets it, and transmits control signals to input/output devices until the necessary operation is accurately executed by the ALU and memory. The Control Unit is a component of the central processing unit that orchestrates the operations of the processor. It directs the computer's memory, arithmetic and logic unit, and input and output devices on how to execute the processor's commands. The computer components receive signals from the control unit to execute instructions. It is also referred to as the central nervous system, or the brain of the computer.
- **Memory Registers:** A register is a compact, ephemeral memory component within the CPU. The processor utilizes it to retain data that it is presently processing. Registers are available in several sizes, including 16-bit, 32-bit, and 64-bit, each serving a distinct function. Some store data, some store instructions, while some retain memory addresses. The Accumulator (ACC) is a crucial register within the CPU. It contains one of the values utilized in computations within the Arithmetic and Logic Unit (ALU). In addition to registers, the internal memory, often known as primary or main memory, temporarily stores the data and instructions during program execution. This memory is referred to as the Random Access Memory (RAM). Each data element in RAM is assigned a distinct address, enabling the CPU to access it swiftly without the need to scan the entire memory. RAM is termed Random Access Memory because it allows immediate access to any data location. The Memory Unit serves as the principal storage component of the computer. It retains both data and instructions. Data and instructions are permanently kept in this unit for immediate accessibility when needed.
- **Output Unit:** The output unit comprises devices connected to the computer for output purposes. It translates the binary data from the CPU into a comprehensible format for humans. The prevalent output devices include monitors, printers, and plotters. The output unit presents or reproduces the processed data in an accessible format for users. It is created by connecting the output devices of a computer. The output unit receives data from the CPU, and presents it in a format comprehensible to the user.
- **Motherboard:** The motherboard serves as the central hub of a computer, interlinking essential components such as the CPU, memory, and storage. It facilitates power distribution, information transfer, and device connectivity,

including peripherals such as a mouse, keyboard, or monitor. A computer specialist may open the PC to inspect for any loose or damaged connections, such as corrosion, if there is an issue with the motherboard. They may also examine the power supply to verify that the computer is receiving electricity correctly.

- **Random Access Memory (RAM):** RAM serves as the computer's ephemeral memory, temporarily housing data while applications are operational. For instance, upon opening an application, it is loaded into RAM, facilitating rapid access by the computer. A specialist is proficient in identifying the type of RAM in a computer, replacing it if found defective, and resolving data transfer issues within memory. They comprehend several forms of RAM and prevalent issues that may impact it. Prior to repairing RAM, a technician may back up essential files to avert the loss of critical programs or documents.
- **Power Supply Unit (PSU):** The Power Supply Unit (PSU) provides electrical power to all components of a computer. It typically links the computer to a wall outlet via a power cable. In the event of a malfunction, a technician may diagnose the issue by powering down the computer, disconnecting the power cord, or testing an alternative cord or socket to ascertain whether the fault is with the power supply or not.
- **Attributes of a Computer Velocity:** Computers can do millions of computations per second. The processing speed is quite rapid.

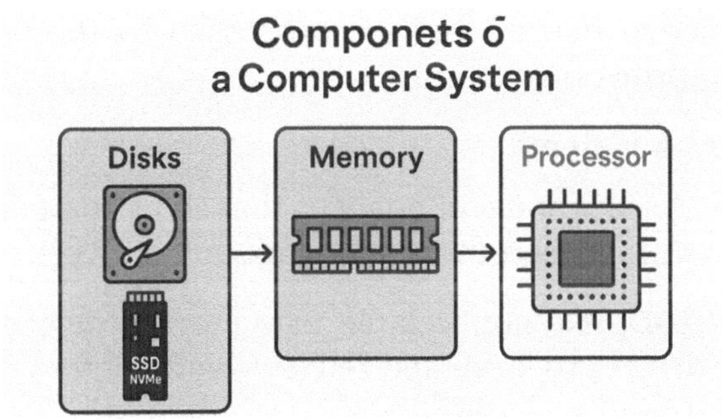

Figure 1.1: *Components of a Computer*

Main Components of a Computer System:

- **Hardware**

  Hardware refers to the physical parts of a computer that you can see and touch. It includes:

  - **Input Devices**: Allow users to enter data into the computer (such as keyboard, mouse, and scanner).
  - **Output Devices**: Display or output information to the user (which includes monitor, printer, or, speakers).

   - **Storage Devices**: Store data permanently or temporarily (namely the hard drive, SSD, and USB flash drive).
   - **Processing Unit (CPU)**: The brain of the computer that processes instructions and performs calculations.
   - **Memory (RAM)**: Temporary storage that holds data and instructions while the computer is running.

- **Software**

  Software is a set of instructions or programs that tell the hardware what to do. It includes:

   - **System Software**: Manages hardware and provides a platform for running application software (includes operating systems such as Windows or Linux).
   - **Application Software**: Programs designed to perform specific tasks for the users (such as word processors, browsers, or games).

- **Peopleware (Users)**

  The users or operators of the computer system. They interact with the system to perform various tasks and make decisions.

- **Data**

  The raw facts and figures that are processed by the computer to produce meaningful information.

- **Networking Components**

  These include devices and technologies that allow computers to communicate with each other, such as routers, modems, and network cards.

A **Hard Disk Drive (HDD)** is a non-volatile data storage device used in computers and other electronic devices to store and retrieve digital information using magnetic storage.

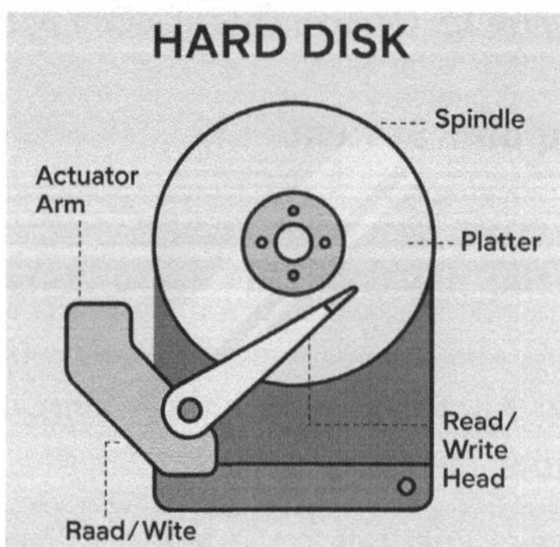

Figure 1.2: *Structure of a Hard Disk Drive*

Key Features:

- **Structure:** Consists of one or more **spinning disks** (called platters) coated with magnetic material. These platters rotate at high speeds (typically 5400 or 7200 RPM in consumer devices).
- **Read/Write Head:** A small actuator arm with read/write heads moves over the platters to access data. It floats just above the surface on a cushion of air.
- **Magnetic Storage:** Data is stored magnetically in binary format (0s and 1s), making it persistent even when the device is powered off.
- **Interface:** Connects to the computer via interfaces like **Serial ATA (Serial ATA),** or older **IDE** standards.

Advantages:

- **Large Storage Capacity:** Commonly available in sizes from 500 GB to 10+ TB.
- **Cost-Effective:** Lower cost per gigabyte as compared to SSDs.

Disadvantages:

- **Slower Speed:** Slower data access and boot times compared to SSDs.
- **Mechanical Parts:** More prone to failure due to moving components.
- **Heavier and Noisier:** Not ideal for portable or silent computing environments.

Common Uses:

- Desktop and laptop computers (especially budget models)
- External backup drives
- Data centers and servers (for bulk storage)

Operating System

An operating system is a piece of software that handles the administration of the hardware that is found in a computer. It acts as a mediator between the user of the computer and the hardware, creating a basis for the application programs, and also serving as a foundation for them. It is quite remarkable that operating systems can perform a wide variety of functions, which is one of its most amazing characteristics. The primary purpose of mainframe operating systems is to make the most of the hardware. Operating systems for Personal Computers (PCs) make it possible to run complex games, commercial software, and a wide variety of other applications. The purpose of the operating systems that are designed for portable computers is to make it easier for the users to interface with the device in order to execute the programs. Consequently, some operating systems are designed to be convenient, while others are designed to be efficient, and yet others are designed to be a combination of these two characteristics. In order to properly comprehend the structure of the computer system, it is necessary to first get an understanding of the intricate workings of the system. To get started, we will investigate its essential functions, which include input/output, storage, and initialization function. In addition, we shall provide an outline of the fundamental computer architecture that is necessary for the development of an operating system that is functional. Considering the significant complexity of an operating system, its development must be carried out in steps that are incremental. Every component must be able to accurately represent a distinct section of the system, complete with inputs, outputs, and functions that have been properly established. In this chapter, a comprehensive overview of the primary components that make up an operating system is presented.

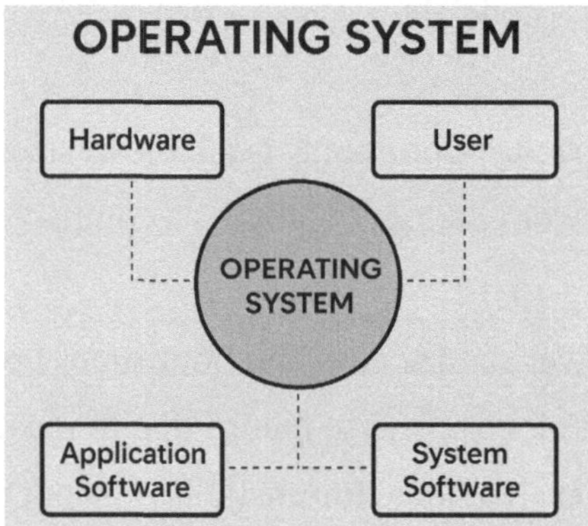

Figure 1.3: *Structure of an Operating System*

Batch Operating System

One of the earliest forms of operating systems—a Batch Operating System is mostly utilized in mainframe computers. It is also one of the oldest types totals. It was designed to carry out a sequence of tasks (programs) in an automated fashion, without requiring any involvement from a human.

- **Example:** IBM OS/360
- **Used in:** Early computing, large mainframes.

Time-Sharing (Multitasking) Operating System

The Time-Sharing Operating System, which is also known as a Multitasking Operating System, is a type of operating system that enables numerous users or processes to use the system at the same time by swiftly switching the CPU between them. There is a little "time slice" of CPU time allocated to each user or job.

- **Example:** UNIX, Linux, Windows (modern versions)
- **Used in:** Multi-user systems, general computing.

Distributed Operating System

A Distributed Operating System, sometimes known as a DOS, is a type of a computer operating system that controls a network of separate computers and displays them to the user as a single, unified system. The purpose is to ensure that the sharing of resources, coordination, and transparency are uninterrupted across a number of different machines.

- **Example:** LOCUS, Amoeba
- **Used in:** Networked environments, cloud computing.

Network Operating System

Computers are able to connect with one another, exchange files, printers, and other devices over a Local Area Network (LAN) or larger networks, thanks to a piece of software known as the Network Operating System (NOS). This software is responsible for managing network resources. On the other hand, with a Network Operating System (NOS), every machine has its own Operating System (OS), and network communication is placed on top of that for the purpose of resource sharing and connectivity.

- **Example:** Novell NetWare, Windows Server
- **Used in:** Servers, enterprise networks.

Real-Time Operating System

As a result of its ability to analyse data and respond to inputs within a predetermined amount of time, a Real-Time Operating System (RTOS) is exceptionally well-suited systems in which timing is of the utmost importance. In embedded systems, when delays or unpredictability can lead to a failure or hazard, it is frequently employed that this technology be used.

- **Example:** VxWorks, FreeRTOS, RTLinux
- **Used in:** Embedded systems, robotics, medical devices.

Mobile Operating System

A Mobile Operating System is a type of operating system that is meant to run on mobile devices such as smartphones, tablets, and other portable devices, including mobile phones. It is possible for the users to interact with the device and run programs as a result of the software platform and the interface that it provides.

- **Example:** Android, iOS
- **Used in:** Mobile and smart devices.

Embedded Operating System

When it comes to embedded systems, which are computing devices that are a component of a larger system or product and typically have dedicated functionality, an embedded operating system, also known as an embedded OS, is a specialized operating system that was built exclusively for embedded systems. It is common for these systems to carry out particular activities, frequently with real-time limitations, and they are designed to function continuously with a high degree of dependability and a minimum amount of resource consumption. An embedded operating system, in contrast to general-purpose operating systems such as Windows or Linux, is tailored for particular hardware, restricted resources (central processing unit, memory, and storage), and unique, specialized use cases.

- **Example:** QNX, Embedded Linux, Windows IoT
- **Used in:** Appliances, cars, industrial machines.

Multi-User and Single-User Operating Systems

As its name suggests, a Single-user Operating System is intended for use by a single individual at a time. Due to the fact that these systems are designed for individual use, it is not possible for several users to access them at the same time. Although the system may be capable of multitasking, which means it may execute numerous programs at the same time, it can only serve a single user at any given time.

- **Multi-user:** Allows multiple users to access the computer simultaneously. *Example: UNIX, Windows Server*
- **Single-user:** Designed for one user at a time. *Example: Windows 10, macOS*

Multiprocessing Operating System

An operating system that can support and manage many Central Processing Units (CPUs) simultaneously within a single computer system is referred to as a Multiprocessing Operating System (MPU OS). There is an increase in the system's performance, efficiency, and reliability because of its capacity to support parallel processing by several processors. It is an usual practice to employ this kind of operating system in settings that call for a significant amount of processing capacity, such as scientific computers, enterprise servers, and contemporary multi-core systems.

- **Example:** Linux, Windows Server with multiple CPUs
- **Used in:** High-performance computing.

Compilers

A Compiler is a software application that converts high-level programming languages, such as C, C++, or Java, into machine language (binary code) that a computer can comprehend and execute.

This translation occurs prior to the program execution, resulting in an executable file. This enables the software to execute swiftly and autonomously from the original source code.

Function of Compiler:

- **Translation:** Transforms source code into machine code.
- **Error Checking:** Identifies syntactic and semantic issues prior to execution.
- **Optimization:** Enhances the code performance and efficiency.
- **Code Generation:** Generates an executable program.

Interpreter

An Interpreter is a program that executes code sequentially, converting high-level programming language into machine code during runtime, rather than compiling the full code simultaneously.

Assembler

An Assembler is a program that converts assembly language, a low-level human-readable format of machine instructions, into a machine code, which consists of binary instructions executable by a CPU.

It is a low-level computer language that does not use binary, but instead, uses mnemonics such as MOV, ADD, and SUB. Computers can only read machine code, which is made up of 0s and 1s. An assembler fills in the blanks.

Algorithm

An Algorithm is a systematic technique, or a collection of clearly specified instructions for addressing a particular problem or executing a task. It receives an input, executes a series of logical operations, and generates an output respectively.

An algorithm is a clearly delineated sequence of instructions intended to execute a given activity or resolve a particular issue. To qualify as an algorithm, a process must demonstrate the following essential characteristics:

Characteristic of an Algorithm:

- **Finiteness:** After a certain number of steps, the algorithm must exit. There must be a termination point; it cannot go forever.
- **Definiteness:** There needs to be a crystal-clear definition of each step. There should be no room for interpretation in the instructions.
- **Input:** An algorithm may possess zero or more inputs. Inputs are the values supplied externally prior to or during the execution of the algorithm.
- **Output:** An algorithm must generate a minimum of one output. The output is the consequence of processing the input via the algorithm.
- **Effectiveness:** Each process must be sufficiently fundamental to be executed, in theory, by an individual utilising solely paper and pencil. All processes must be practical and not excessively intricate.
- **Generality:** The algorithm needs to be appropriate to a category of issues rather than a singular special instance. It must yield accurate results for all valid inputs within the given problem domain.

Example of Algorithm: Find the Largest of Three Numbers

Step 1: Start

Step 2: Input three numbers: A, B, and C

Step 3: If A ≥ B and A ≥ C

then

Print A is the largest

Step 4: Else if B ≥ A and B ≥ C,

then

print B is the largest

Step 5: Else

print C is the largest

Step 6: End

Aspect	Algorithm	Flowchart
Definition	A detailed set of instructions for completing a task or resolving an issue.	A visual representation of the stages of a process or algorithm through the use of symbols.
Form	Pseudocode or straightforward language.	Displayed graphically using standardised shapes (for example, diamonds, rectangles).
Understandability	Needs a logical comprehension and interpretation of the instructions.	Visual representation facilitates comprehension.
Representation	A representation of logic that is text-based.	Diagrammatic or graphical representation.
Usage	Used for coding, problem-solving, and logical thinking.	Used for designing and explaining processes visually.
Modification	Easier to edit and update.	More time-consuming to revise, especially in complex diagrams.
Tool Requirement	Does not require any specific tools—can be written on paper or digitally.	Often requires diagramming tools or software for neat presentation.

Table 1.1: *Difference between Flowchart and Algorithm*

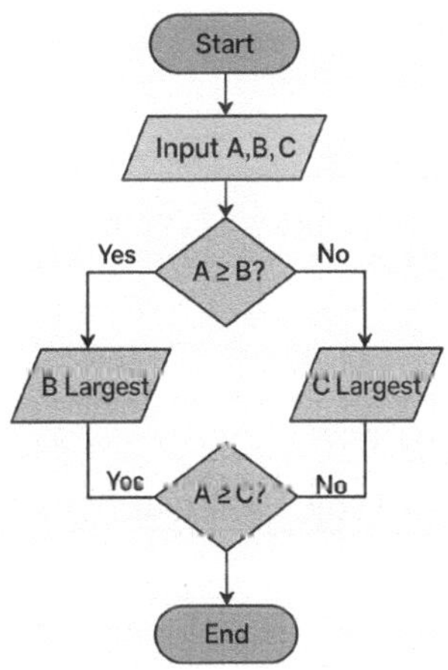

Figure 1.4: *Largest of Three Numbers Flowchart*

Variable:

A memory location that stores data is referred to as a variable. The value of a variable may fluctuate during the execution of a program.

Syntax:

```
data_typevariable_name;
```

Example:

```
int length = 25;
float breadth = 5.9;
char height = 'A';
```

Rules for Creating Variables:

- Must begin with a letter (A-Z or a-z) or underscore _.
- Can contain letters, digits (0–9), and underscores.
- Case sensitive (age and Age are different).
- Cannot be a reserved keyword (such as int, return, and so on).

Data Type:

The type of data that a variable can store is determined by its data types. It instructs the compiler on the amount of space to allocate and the types of operations that can be performed on the data.

Basic Data Types in C:

Data Type	Description	Size (Typical)	Example
int	Integer values	4 bytes	int x = 10;
float	Decimal numbers	4 bytes	float y = 3.5;
double	Double-precision float	8 bytes	double z = 3.14159;
char	Single character	1 byte	char c = 'A';

Table 1.2: *Description of Primitive Data Types*

Format Specifiers:

Used in **`printf ()`** and **`scanf ()`** for input/output:

Data Type	Format Specifier
int	%d
float	%f
double	%lf
char	%c

Table 1.3: *Description of Primitive Data Types and Format Specifiers*

Example

```
#include <stdio.h>
int main() {
    int age = 20;
    float weight = 65.5;
    char grade = 'B';

    printf("Age: %d\n", age);
    printf("Weight: %.2f\n", weight);
    printf("Grade: %c\n", grade);

    return 0;
}
```

Figure 1.5: *Code Window*

Output Window:

```
C:\Users\Dipra Mitra\Docume

Age: 20
Weight: 65.50
Grade: B

--------------------------------
Process exited after 0.09616 seconds with return value 0
Press any key to continue . . .
```

Figure 1.6: *Output Window*

Figure 1.5 illustrates the execution of a C program and how to declare variables, data types, and library functions, and *Figure* 1.6 illustrates the output window. **`#include`** is a preprocessor directive in C that instructs the compiler to incorporate the Standard Input Output header file before compiling the actual code.

Conclusion

The first chapter of C programming provides a foundational understanding of the language, its structure, and its significance in modern computing. It introduces the history of C, its importance in system-level programming, and the basic structure of a C program.

The chapter has also explained essential programming concepts such as variables, data types, format specifiers, and input/output functions. In addition, the fundamental components of a computer system are discussed to help learners understand how C interacts with hardware and system resources.

Overall, this chapter establishes a strong base in both programming fundamentals, and computer concepts, preparing learners to write simple C programs, and advance toward more complex programming topics in the subsequent chapters.

Exercises

Theory Questions

1. What is the structure of a basic C program?
2. What are the main components of a C program?
3. Explain the purpose of the **`main()`** function in C.
4. What is the use of **`#include<stdio.h>`**?
5. What is the difference between a compiler and an interpreter?
6. Define keywords, identifiers, and constants in C.
7. What are variables in C? How do you declare them?
8. What are the rules for naming identifiers in C?
9. What are data types? List the basic data types in C.
10. What is the difference between int, float, char, and double?

Practical/Programming Questions

1. Write a C program to print "Hello, World!" on the screen.
2. Write a program to add two numbers entered by the user.
3. Write a C program to find the area of a circle given its radius.
4. Write a program to swap two numbers using a third variable.
5. Write a C program to convert temperature from Celsius to Fahrenheit.
6. Write a program to print your name, age, and grade.
7. Write a C program to calculate simple interest.
8. Write a program that takes an integer input from the user and prints whether it is positive, negative, or zero.
9. Write a program to calculate the sum and average of three numbers.
10. Write a program to find the square and cube of a number.

Chapter 2
Arithmetic Expressions and Precedence

Introduction

Arithmetic expressions and their precedence are a basic aspect of programming in C and other languages. These ideas enable programmers to execute mathematical operations utilising a mix of values (operands) and arithmetic operators, including addition, subtraction, multiplication, and division. An arithmetic expression is a series of operands and operators that the compiler assesses to yield a numerical outcome. The precise interpretation and assessment of these expressions are crucial for accurate computations and logical progression in a program. Operator precedence denotes the regulations that dictate the sequence in which operators are assessed within an expression. As with conventional mathematics, certain operations take precedence over others unless modified by brackets. For example, multiplication and division are prioritised above addition and subtraction. Comprehending these regulations facilitates the composition of efficient and error-free code. This subject is necessary for establishing a robust foundation in programming logic, allowing students and developers to devise dependable and accurate computational solutions.

Structure

- Identifiers
- Types
- Constants
- Symbolic Constants
- Declarations

Identifiers

Identifiers, such as variable and function names, consist of letters and digits, and are case-sensitive. The initial character of an identifier must be a letter or an underscore (_).

The C language comprises of 32 reserved keywords that cannot be used as identifiers (namely int, while). Moreover, it is advisable to refrain from redefining identifiers used by the C standard library, including standard function names.

As a stylistic convention, use lowercase for variable identifiers and uppercase for symbolic constants. Local variable names should be concise, whereas external names should be longer and more descriptive. Variable names may begin with an underscore (_); however, this practice is discouraged because such names are conventionally reserved for library implementations.

Types

C is a statically typed language. Each variable is assigned a specific type that delineates the values it can represent, the manner in which its data is stored in memory, and the actions that can be executed on it. By mandating that the programmer explicitly provide a type for all variables and interfaces, the type system empowers the compiler to identify type-mismatch mistakes, thus averting a substantial source of faults.

The C language comprises of three fundamental types: characters, integers, and floating-point numbers.

Sizes may differ across various platforms. Almost all contemporary devices represent an integer with a minimum of 32 bits, and many currently utilise 64 bits. The size of an int typically denotes the machine's natural word size, which is the native dimension utilised by the CPU for processing instructions and data.

The standard specifies that a short int must be a minimum of 16 bits, a long int must be a minimum of 32 bits, and the relationship short int < int ≤ long int must hold.

The standard specifies no details regarding the size of floating-point numbers, other than the hierarchy: float ≤ double ≤ long double.

A software that displays the range of values for specific data formats is presented in the succeeding code. Parameters like **INT_MIN** are located in the standard header limitations. **h** and **float.h**

```
#include <stdio.h>
#include <limits.h>
#include <float.h>

int main(void)
```

```
{
printf("Integer range:\t%d to %d\n", INT_MIN, INT_MAX);
printf("Long range:\t%ld to %ld\n", LONG_MIN, LONG_MAX);
printf("Float range:\t%e to %e\n", FLT_MIN, FLT_MAX);
printf("Double range:\t%e to %e\n", DBL_MIN, DBL_MAX);
printf("Long double range:\t%e to %e\n", LDBL_MIN, LDBL_MAX);
printf("Float-Double epsilon:\t%e %e\n", FLT_EPSILON, DBL_EPSILON);

    return 0;
}
```

The size of a type in characters, often corresponding to the number of bytes, can be determined using the **sizeof** operator. This operator is not a function; rather, it is a keyword, despite frequently resembling one. It yields an unsigned integer of type **size_t**, as defined in the header file **stddef.h**.

```
#include <stdio.h>

int main(void)
{
printf("void\tchar\tshort\tint\tlong\tfloat\tdouble\n");
printf("%3zu\t%3zu\t%3zu\t%3zu\t%3zu\t%3zu\t%3zu\n",
sizeof(void),
sizeof(char),
sizeof(short),
sizeof(int),
sizeof(long),
sizeof(float),
sizeof(double));

    return 0;
}
```

The terms short and long are referred to as the type qualifiers, as they influence the size of the fundamental int type. The qualifier long can also be applied to the double type It is important to note that the terms short and long, when utilised independently as in short a; long x; are synonymous with the expressions short int and long int, respectively. Additional type qualifiers include signed, unsigned, const, and volatile. The qualifiers, whether signed or unsigned, can be applied to char or any integer type. A signed type can denote negative values; the Most Significant Bit (MSB) serves as the sign bit, and the value is generally represented in two's complement binary format. An unsigned type is inherently non-negative, with the most significant bit contributing to the numerical value, hence doubling the maximum representable value relative to a comparable signed type. A 16-bit signed short may represent integers from –32768 to 32767 (such as, -2^{15} to 2^{15-1}), but a 16-bit unsigned short can represent integers from 0 to 65535 (such as, 0 to 2^{16-1}).

Note: *Integer types are signed by default (for example, declaring short is synonymous with declaring signed short int). Nonetheless, the default designation of plain chars as signed or unsigned is contingent upon the system architecture.*

The qualifier const indicates that the associated variable is immutable.

```
const int DoesNotChange = 5;
DoesNotChange = 6;    /* Error: compilation failure */
```

The term volatile, pertains to variables whose values may fluctuate in ways that beyond the program's standard control mechanisms. This is pertinent to multi-threaded programming or hardware interfacing, subjects that exceed the scope of this text. The volatile qualifier is not pertinent to standard-conforming C programs and will not be discussed further in this work. Lastly, there exists a type known as void, which denotes a "no value" type. It serves as an argument for functions devoid of parameters and as a return type for functions that yield no value.

Constants

Constants may possess several forms and representations. This section illustrates several sorts of constants with examples. An integer constant 1234 is classified as type int. A constant of type long int is suffixed with an L, such as 1234L; integer constants beyond the size of int are implicitly treated as long. An unsigned integer is denoted with a U suffix, as in 1234U, while UL indicates an unsigned long.

Integer constants can be represented using octal (base 8) or hexadecimal (base 16) numbers, instead of decimal (base 10). Octal numerals are denoted by a leading 0, while hexadecimal numbers are indicated by 0x. Consequently, 1234 in decimal is equivalent to 02322 in octal and 0x4D2 in hexadecimal. It is essential to note that these three constants denote precisely the same value (0101 1101 0010 in binary). For instance, let us consider the subsequent code:

```
int x = 1234, y = 02322, z = 0x4D2;
printf("%d\t%o\t%x\n", x, x, x);
printf("%d\t%d\t%d\n", x, y, z);
```

It prints:

```
1234    2322    4d2
1234    1234    1234
```

Figure 2.1: *Output of the above Code*

Observe that C does not offer a straight binary representation. Nevertheless, the hexadecimal format is highly practical as it decomposes binary into groups of four bits Floating-point constants are denoted by the presence of a decimal point following a numeral. For instance, 1. and 1.3 are classified as double, 3.14f and 2.f are categorised as float, whereas 7.L is designated as long double. Floating-point numbers may also be expressed in scientific notation, for instance, 1.65e-2 (which corresponds to 0.0165). Constant expressions, exemplified as 3+7+9.2, are computed at compile-time and substituted with a singular constant value, 19.2. Consequently, constant expressions entail no runtime overhead. Character constants, such as '**a**', '**\n**', and '**7**', are denoted by single quotation marks. Character constants are significant since they are of type int rather than char. Consequently, size of('Z') will equal 4 on a 32-bit computer, rather than one. Most platforms utilise the ASCII character set, which correlates integers 0 to 127 with designated characters (for instance the character 'T' corresponds to the value 84). Most platforms use the ASCII character set, which maps integers from 0 to 127 to specific characters (for example, the character 'T' corresponds to the value 84). ASCII tables clearly show this mapping. Some characters, however, cannot be displayed or typed directly; these are represented using escape sequences such as **\n** (newline) or **\t** (tab). It is essential to acknowledge that these escape characters still denote individual characters. A collection of essential escape characters includes the following:

\0 represents NUL (used to terminate character strings),

\n denotes newline,

\t signifies tab,

\v indicates vertical tab,

\\ stands for backslash,

\' refers to single quotes, \" corresponds to double quotes, and **\b** represents backspace. String constants, exemplified as "This is a string," are enclosed in quotation marks (the quotation marks are not integral to the string constant). They are implicitly suffixed with a terminating '\0' character. Consequently, in memory, the string constant would consist of the subsequent character sequence.

Symbolic Constants

Symbolic constants denote constant values from the aforementioned collection of constant types using a symbolic identifier.

For example,

```
#define BLOCK_SIZE 100
 #define TRACK_SIZE (16*BLOCK_SIZE)
 #define HELLO "Hello World\n"
#define EXP 2.7183
```

Whenever a symbolic constant is encountered in the code, it is equivalent to a straight textual substitution with the defined constant. For instance,

```
Print("hello world")
```

The string "Hello World" is printed. One reason to use symbolic constants instead of directly using numeric values is to prevent the spread of “magic numbers,” which are numerical constants scattered throughout the code. Magic numbers are prone to errors, and make the program difficult to modify or maintain. Symbolic constants, on the other hand, are defined in one place, making changes easier and safer.

In C, symbolic constants can be defined using the **#define** preprocessor directive. Like **#include**, it is handled before compilation and follows the rules which are different from the main C language. The **#** symbol must appear at the beginning of a line and should not be indented.

Another way to create symbolic constants is by using an enumeration. An enumeration is a list of named integer constants.

For example:

```
enum Boolean { FALSE, TRUE };
```

The enumeration tag Boolean defines a new type, and variables of this type can take the values **FALSE** or **TRUE**.

By default, the values in an enumeration start at 0 and increase by 1 for each member (for example, **FALSE** is **0** and **TRUE** is 1). However, explicit values may also be assigned. For instance:

```
enum { RED = 2, GREEN = 4, BLUE, YELLOW = 4, BLACK };
int y = BLUE;
```

If an enumeration is declared without a tag, its members are still of type int. When explicit values are assigned, each unspecified member takes a value greater than the previous one.

printf Conversion Specifiers

The standard function **printf()** facilitates formatted text output. It merges numerical values of any type into a character string using various formatting operators and conversion specifiers.

```
printf("Character values %c %c %c\n", ’a’, ’b’, ’c’);
printf("Some floating-point values %f %f %f\n", 3.556, 2e3, 40.1f);
printf("Scientific notation %e %e %e\n", 3.556, 2e3, 40.1f);
printf("%15.10s\n", "Hello World\n"); /* Right-justify string with space
for 15 chars, print only first 10 letters */
```

Declarations

Every variable must be declared before it is used. A declaration specifies the variable’s type and name, and it may optionally assign an initial value. In C, variables are typically declared at the beginning of a block, which is a section of code enclosed within curly braces { }.

Following are some examples of variable declarations:

```
{   /* beginning of a block */

    int lower, upper, step;          /* three uninitialized integers */
    char tab = '\t';                 /* a character initialized with '\t'
*/
    char buf[10];                    /* an uninitialized character array
*/
    int m = 2 + 3 * 4;               /* constant expression: 14 */
    int n = m + 5;                   /* initialized using another variable
*/
    float limit = 9.34f;
const double PI = 3.1416;
}
```

The general form of a declaration is:

```
type variable_name = value;
```

Arithmetic Operations

You can choose between two types of arithmetic operators: unary and binary. The plus (+), minus (-), multiply (*), divide (/), and modulus (%) operators are the binary operators.

You can use the first four operators with either integers or floating-point numbers. However, keep in mind that integer division discards any fractional part (for example, 17 / 5 is equal to 3).

The modulus operator (%) works only with integer types (such as char and int) and gives the remainder when one integer is divided by another. For example, 18 % 7 gives 4.

For negative numbers, the behavior of / and % may depend on the platform.

The plus (+) and minus (-) symbols can also act as unary operators. The unary plus (+x) returns the value unchanged, while the unary minus (-x) changes the sign of the value.

The increment (++) and decrement (--) operators increase or decrease a variable by 1.

In this case, x++ means the same as x = x + 1.

The operators ++ and -- can be used either before or after a variable, but they behave differently.

For example:

```
double x = 3.2;
double y = ++x;
double z = x++;
```

In the first case (pre-increment), x is increased before it is assigned to y.

In the second case (post-increment), the original value of x is assigned first, and then x is increased.

The order of precedence for arithmetic operators is as follows:

1. Unary operators (++, --, unary +, unary -)
2. Multiplication, division, and modulus (*, /, %)
3. Addition and subtraction (+, -)

For example:

```
int a = 2, b = 7, c = 5, d = 9;
printf("a*b + c*d = %d\n", a*b + c*d);  /* prints 59 */
```

When working with numbers, divide-by-zero and overflow are two common runtime errors. Divide-by-zero occurs when a value is divided by zero. Overflow occurs when the result of an operation exceeds the maximum value that can be represented by the data type.

For example:

```
int z = x + 1;
```

If x is already the largest representable value of type int, this operation may result in overflow. The resulting value may be incorrect and can vary across platforms.

Working of Relational Operators

```
#include <stdio.h>

int main()
{
    int x = 5, y = 5, z = 10;

printf("%d == %d is %d\n", x, y, x == y);
printf("%d == %d is %d\n", x, z, x == z);
printf("%d > %d is %d\n", x, y, x > y);
printf("%d > %d is %d\n", x, z, x > z);
printf("%d < %d is %d\n", x, y, x < y);
printf("%d < %d is %d\n", x, z, x < z);
printf("%d != %d is %d\n", x, y, x != y);
```

```
printf("%d != %d is %d\n", x, z, x != z);
printf("%d >= %d is %d\n", x, y, x >= y);
printf("%d >= %d is %d\n", x, z, x >= z);
printf("%d <= %d is %d\n", x, y, x <= y);
printf("%d <= %d is %d\n", x, z, x <= z);

    return 0;
}
```

Relational and Logical Operations

- There are six relational operators: greater-than **>**, less-than **<**, less-than-or-equal-to **<=**, greater-than-or-equal-to **>=**, equal-to **==**, and not-equal-to **!=**. Relational expressions evaluate to 1 if they are TRUE and 0 if they are FALSE. For example, 2.1 < 7 evaluates to 1, and x != x evaluates to 0.

  Note: A *very common programming error is mistakenly typing* `=` *(assignment) instead of* `==` *(equality).*

  For example, consider a loop that is intended to execute while x == 3.

  Consider this code:

  ```
  while (x = 3)
          {
                      /* various statements here */
          }
  ```

  Here, **x** will be assigned the value 3, and this value will become the loop condition. Since 3 is non-zero (and therefore **TRUE**), the loop will execute indefinitely, resulting in an infinite loop.

  The three logical operators are AND **&&**, OR **||**, and NOT **!**. All relational and logical operators are binary except the **!** operator, which is unary. The && and || operators connect pairs of conditional expressions, with **&&** being TRUE only if both expressions are TRUE, and **||** being TRUE if at least one expression is TRUE. They can be used to chain multiple expressions together, as in the following example where the integer values are a = 1, b = 2, c = 3, and d = 3.

  ```
  (a < b && b < c && c < d)       /* FALSE */
  (a < b && b < c && c <= d)      /* TRUE */
  ((a < b && b < c) || c < d)     /* TRUE */
  ```

  The **&&** and **||** operators are evaluated from left to right, and evaluation stops as soon as the final result is determined. The remaining expressions are not evaluated. This feature is known as short-circuit evaluation.

For instance, if you have an array of length **SIZE**, you should not access **array[SIZE]**, which is one position beyond the end of the array.

The following statement ensures that **array[i]** is not evaluated when **i == SIZE**.

:

```
i = 0;
        while (i< SIZE && array[i] != val)
   ++i;
```

The unary operator **!** changes a non-zero value to 0 and a zero value to 1.

For example:

```
if (!valid)
            x = y;
```

This statement assigns x to y only if valid is 0.

The **!** operator should be used carefully, as excessive use can reduce code readability.

In terms of operator precedence, arithmetic operators have higher precedence than relational and logical operators. Among the relational and logical operators, the order of precedence is:

1. !
2. >, <, >=, <=
3. ==, !=
4. &&
5. ||

Example of Operator Precedence

```
#include <stdio.h>

int main() {
    int a = 10;
    int b = 5;
    int c = 2;
    int result;

    // Example 1: Multiplication has higher precedence than addition
    result = a + b * c;
printf("Result of a + b * c: %4d\n", result);

    // Example 2: Parentheses override precedence
    result = (a + b) * c;
printf("Result of (a + b) * c: %4d\n", result);
```

```
    // Example 3: Division has higher precedence than subtraction
    result = a - b / c;
printf("Result of a - b / c: %4d\n", result);

    // Example 4: Logical AND (&&) has higher precedence than Logical OR
(||)
    result = (a > b && b < c) || a >c;
printf("Result of (a > b && b < c) || a > c: %4d\n", result);

    return 0;
}
```

Explanation

In Example 1, **`b * c`** is evaluated first because multiplication (*****) has higher precedence than addition (**+**). The result is 10 + 10 = 20.

In Example 2, the parentheses force a + b to be evaluated first. Thus, (10 + 5) * 2 = 30.

In Example 3, division (**/**) has higher precedence than subtraction (**-**). Since b and c are integers, 5 / 2 evaluates to 2 (integer division). Therefore, 10 - 2 = 8.

In Example 4, the logical AND operator (**&&**) has higher precedence than the logical OR operator (**||**). First, (**`a > b && b < c`**) is evaluated. Since 10 > 5 is true and 5 < 2 is false, the result is false. Then false **||** (10 > 2) becomes false **||** true, which evaluates to true (1).

Bitwise Operators

There are several bitwise functions in C that let you work with single bits, or binary 1s and 0s. You need these to do a low-level code, like handling hardware. We shall discuss in detail about bitwise operators in Chapter 12, but we will mention them here, so that they do not get mixed up with the logical operators, which they look a lot like. They are: bitwise AND (**&**), bitwise OR (**|**), bitwise exclusive OR (^), left shift (<<), right shift (>>), and one's complement (^). & is not the same as **&&**, **|** is not the same as **||**, and >> does not mean "much greater than." The logical operator and the bitwise operator are used for very different things, and cannot be used in place of each other.

```
#include <stdio.h>

int main() {

    int a = 12, b = 25;

printf("Bitwise AND (a & b) = %d\n", a & b);
printf("Bitwise OR (a | b) = %d\n", a | b);
printf("Bitwise XOR (a ^ b) = %d\n", a ^ b);
```

```
    int num = 212, i;

    for (i = 0; i<= 2; ++i) {
printf("Right shift by %d: %d\n", i, num>>i);
    }

printf("\n");

    for (i = 0; i<= 2; ++i) {
printf("Left shift by %d: %d\n", i, num<<i);
    }

    return 0;
}
```

Assignment Operator: A lot of the time, the assignment operator **=** is used with the math or bitwise operators; taking for example, z = x + y. There are times when the variable on the left is repeated right away on the right (for instance, x = x + y). The short form for these kinds of expressions is x += y. The plus sign (+=) is known as the assignment operator. The assignment operators that go with the binary math operators **+**, **-**, *****, **/**, and **%** are **+=**, **-=**, ***=**, **/=**, and **%=**. This means we do not have to write x = x * (y + 1), but x * = y + 1. In addition, we are also listing the bitwise assignment operators **&=**, **|=**, **^=**, **<<=**, and **>>=**.

Type Conversions and Casts

A few rules tell the computer what type of operands to use when an operator has operands of different kinds.

If neither operand is unsigned, the following rules apply to a binary expression such as a * b:

- If either operand is a long double, the other operand is converted to long double.
- Otherwise, if either operand is a double, the other is converted to double.
- Otherwise, if either operand is a float, the other is converted to float.
- Operands of type char and short are promoted to int.
- If either operand is long, the other is converted to long.

If two operands have the same type, but one is signed, and the other is unsigned, the signed operand is converted to unsigned. If the signed value is negative, this conversion may produce unexpected results.

The following code shows a simple case of type promotion:

```
Short a = 5, int b = 10, float c = 23.1f, and double d = c + a*b.
```

- Since multiplication has higher precedence, a is first promoted to an int and multiplied by b. The result of this operation is then converted to a float and added to c. Finally, the resulting value is promoted to a double and assigned to d.
- The conversion from char to int depends on the implementation, because a plain char may be either signed or unsigned. If char is signed and its most significant bit is 1, sign extension occurs. If it is unsigned, zero extension occurs, meaning the higher-order bits are filled with zeros and the value remains non-negative.

It is possible to assign to a "narrower" target, but data may be lost. Good processors should give you a warning when you try to convert to a smaller type.

The higher-order bits are truncated when going from a larger integer to a smaller one, and any fractional part is truncated when going from a floating-point number to an integer.

For instance, if you write "**`int iresult = 0.5 + 3/5.0`**," the division by 3/5.0 is turned into a double, which makes the end sum 1.1. In the assignment to iresult, the result is then cut off at 1.

Keep in mind that the way a number is converted from double to float depends on the software used. The number may be reduced or rounded off. You should stay away from narrowing changes. In the situations where they are needed, a cast should make them clear.

As an example, we can write: `int iresult = (int)(0.5 + 3/5.0);`

Cages can also be used to force someone to convert, like when someone breaks the rules for promotions listed above. For instance, the phrase **`result = (float)5.0 + 3.f`**; will add the two numbers as floats instead of doubles.

Example of Type Casting

```
#include<stdio.h>

int main () {

  // create an integer variable
  int number = 97;
printf ("Integer Value: %d\n", number);

  // (char) converts number to character
  char alphabet = (char) number;
printf ("Character Value: %c", alphabet);

  return 0;
}
```

Conclusion

To conclude, knowing arithmetic terms and how they work is essential for writing correct and useful programmes. We can use operations like addition, subtraction, multiplication, division, and modulus to do basic math with arithmetic expressions. The way in which these actions are done is set by the operator precedence and associativity rules. This makes sure that expressions are correctly evaluated. By understanding these ideas, coders can avoid making mistakes in the logic, write a code that is easier to understand, and make their programmes more reliable overall. So, if you want to be a programmer or study computer science, you first need to have a good understanding of arithmetic processes, and the order in which they should be used.

Exercises

Part A: Multiple Choice Questions

1. What is the result of the following expression: 10 + 5 * 2?
    a. 30
    b. 20
    c. 25
    d. 15
2. Which operator has the highest precedence in C language?
    a. + (Addition)
    b. *(Multiplication)
    c. ( ) (Parentheses)
    d. % (Modulus)
3. What is the associativity of the division / operator in C?
    a. Right to Left
    b. Left to Right
    c. Top to Bottom
    d. None
4. Which of the following expressions will be evaluated first?
    a. a + (b * c)
    b. (a + b) * c
    c. a + b * c
    d. All have the same precedence.

Part B: Fill in the Blanks

1. The order in which operators are evaluated in an expression is called ____________.
2. Operators with the same precedence are evaluated based on their ____________.
3. The modulus operator (%) is used to find the ____________ of a division.
4. Parentheses are used in expressions to change the ____________ of evaluation.

Part C: Write the Output

1. Evaluate the expression: 15 - 4 * 2 + 6 / 3
2. What is the result of: 8 + 2 * 3 - (4 + 2)
3. Find the output: (10 + 5) % 4 * 2

Part D: Short Answer Questions

1. Explain the concept of operator precedence with an example.
2. How does associativity affect the evaluation of arithmetic expressions?
3. Write and evaluate an expression using all five arithmetic operators: +, -, *, /, %.
4. Why is it important to use parentheses in complex expressions?

CHAPTER 3
Branching and Iteration

Introduction

To make logical and efficient programs, programmers must be able to manage the flow of execution. Branching and iteration are two important ideas that make this control possible.

Branching is the ability of a software to make decisions. It lets the software choose between two or more ways to run, based on specified conditions. Conditional statements like if, if-else, nested if, or switch-case are usually used to perform this. When a program branches, it can react differently to different inputs or conditions. This is what makes it smart and dynamic. On the other hand, iteration is the process of running a block of code repeatedly. Iteration, which is also called looping, is helpful when you need to do something a certain number of times, or until a certain condition is met. For, while, and do-while loops are some of the most common types of iteration structures. Branching and iteration are the two main parts of logical programming. They let programmers design code that can make choices and do the same thing repeatedly, which makes software solutions more powerful and adaptable.

There are three ways to make decisions in the C language: the if-else statement, the conditional expression, and the switch statement. It also has three ways to loop: while, do-while, and for. Also, it features the renowned "go to," which can branch and loop without any conditions.

Structure

In this chapter, the following topics are discussed in detail:

- Introduction to Branching
- if Statement

- if-else and Nested if
- Conditional (Ternary) Operator
- switch Statement
- Introduction to Loops
- for Loop
- while Loop
- do-while Loop
- Comparison of Loop Structures
- Pre-Increment and Post-Increment Operators
- Practical Programs Using Branching and Looping
- Exercises

Branching

Branching is the ability of a program to execute different blocks of code based on certain conditions. It allows the program to take different paths depending on whether a condition is true or false.

Branching is commonly implemented using:

- if statements
- if-else statements
- nested if-else statements
- switch-case statements
- Conditional (ternary) operator

- **if Statement**

  The if statement is used to make decisions in C. It executes a block of code, only if the given condition is true. If the condition is false, the block is skipped.

  Example:

```
#include<stdio.h>

intmain()
{
int x = 8, y - 9;

if (x > y)
    {
printf("%2d", x);
```

```
    }
if (x < y)
    {
printf("%2d", y);
    }
return0;
}
```

Explanation: In this program, the value of x is 8 and y is 9. Since x < y is true, the second if block executes and prints the value of y. The first if condition is false, so that the block is skipped.

- **Nested if-else**

  A nested if-else statement is an if-else statement placed inside another if or else block. It is used when multiple conditions need to be checked step by step.

  General Structure:

```
if (condition1)
{
if (condition2)
    {
statement;
    }
else
    {
statement;
    }
}
else
{
statement;
}
```

  Example:

```
#include<stdio.h>

int main()
{
    int x, y, z;

printf("Enter three numbers: ");
scanf("%d%d%d", &x, &y, &z);

if (x > y)
```

```
    {
if (x > z)
        {
printf("%d is the greatest", x);
        }
else
        {
printf("%d is the greatest", z);
        }
    }
else
    {
if (y > z)
        {
printf("%d is the greatest", y);
        }
else
        {
printf("%d is the greatest", z);
        }
    }

return0;
}
```

Explanation: This program compares three numbers and prints the greatest among them. First, it compares x and y. Then, it compares the larger value with z to determine the greatest number.

Conditional (ternary) operator

In several programming languages, including C, C++, Java, and JavaScript, an if-else statement can be written concisely by using the conditional (ternary) operator.

Syntax:

condition ? expression_if_true : expression_if_false;

Explanation:

If the **condition is true**, it returns expression_if_true

If the **condition is false**, it returns expression_if_false

Example: To Find out greater number between two numbers

```
#include <stdio.h>

int main() {
```

```
    int a = 10, b = 20;
    int max;

    max = (a > b) ? a : b;

    printf("Maximum = %d", max);
    return 0;
}
Output: Maximum = 20
```

Example: To find out a given number is Even or Odd

```
int main()
{
int num = 5;

(num % 2 == 0) ? printf("Even") : printf("Odd");
}
Output: Odd
```

Example: To find out if a given number is a greater number among three numbers or not.

```
#include <stdio.h>

int main() {
int a = 10, b = 25, c = 15;
int max;

max = (a > b) ? ((a > c) ? a : c) : ((b > c) ? b : c);

printf("Greatest = %d", max);
return 0;
}
```

- **Switch Statement**

  The switch statement is another way to make decisions. It compares the value of a variable or expression with multiple constant values called cases. It is often used instead of long if-else-if chains when checking equality.

  Syntax:

  ```
  switch (expression)
  {
  case constant1:
          // code
  break;

  case constant2:
  ```

```
        // code
break;

default:
        // code
}
```

Example:

```
#include<stdio.h>

int main()
{
    int day = 5;

switch (day)
    {
case 1:
printf("Monday");
break;

case 2:
printf("Tuesday");
break;

case 3:
printf("Wednesday");
break;

default:
printf("Invalid day");
    }

return0;
}
```

Explanation: The value of day is 5. Since there is no case for 5, the default case executes and prints "Invalid day".

Description of for Loop in C Programming: The for loop is a fundamental control structure in C used to execute a block of code repeatedly, especially when the number of iterations is known in advance. It is compact and convenient because it combines initialization, condition checking, and increment/decrement in a single line.

Syntax:

```
for (initialization; condition; increment/decrement) {
    // Statements to be executed
}
```

Components:

- **Initialization**: Sets the starting value of the loop variable (such as int i = 0).
- **Condition**: The loop continues to execute as long as this condition remains true.
- **Increment/Decrement**: Updates the loop variable after each iteration.

Working:

1. The loop begins with an initialization.
2. The condition is evaluated.
3. If the condition is true, the loop body executes.
4. After executing the body, the increment/decrement statement runs.
5. The condition is checked again.
6. The process continues until the condition becomes false.

Example:

```
#include<stdio.h>

int main() {
for (int i = 1; i<= 5; i++) {
printf("Iteration %d\n", i);
    }
return0;
}
```

Output:

```
Iteration 1
Iteration 2
Iteration 3
Iteration 4
Iteration 5
```

Thus, the for loop is widely used for iterating arrays, executing a code for a fixed number of times, and generating patterns.

While Loop

The `while` loop is a control structure that repeatedly executes a block of code as long as a specified condition remains true. Unlike the **`for`** loop, it is commonly used when the number of iterations is not known beforehand.

Syntax:

```
while (condition) {
```

```
    // Statements to be executed
}
```

How It Works:

1. The condition is evaluated before every iteration.
2. If the condition is true, the loop body executes.
3. After execution, the condition is checked again.
4. The loop terminates when the condition becomes false.

Example:

```
#include<stdio.h>

int main() {
    int i = 1;
while (i<= 5) {
printf("%d\n", i);
i++;
    }
return0;
}
```

Output:

```
1
2
3
4
5
```

Key Points:

- The loop may not execute at all if the condition is false at the beginning.
- It is suitable when repetition depends on a condition rather than a fixed count.
- The loop variable must be updated inside the loop to avoid infinite loops.

Do-While Loop

The do-while loop executes a block of code at least once and then continues the execution as long as the specified condition remains true. The key difference is that the condition is checked after the loop body executes.

Syntax:

```
do {
    // Statements to be executed
}while (condition);
```

How It Works:

1. The loop body executes first.
2. The condition is evaluated.
3. If the condition is true, the loop executes again.
4. The process continues until the condition becomes false.

Example:

```
#include<stdio.h>

int main() {
    int i = 1;
do {
printf("%d\n", i);
i++;
    } while (i<= 5);
return0;
}
```

Output:

```
1
2
3
4
5
```

Key Points:

- The do-while loop always executes at least once.
- It is useful when the loop body runs before checking the condition (for example, user input).
- Care must be taken to update the condition properly to prevent infinite loops.

Feature	While Loop	Do-while Loop
Condition Checking	Before executing the loop body (pre-test).	After executing the loop body (post-test).
Minimum Execution	May not execute even once.	Executes at least once.
Syntax	while(condition) {}	do {} while(condition);
Use Case	When condition must be checked first.	When loop must execute at least once.

Table 3.1: *Difference between While Loop and Do-While Loop*

Sample Program to Find the Factorial of a Number

```
#include<stdio.h>

int main() {
    int fact = 1, n, i;

printf("Enter a number: ");
scanf("%d", &n);

for (i = 1; i<= n; i++) {
        fact = fact * i;
    }

printf("The value of factorial is = %d", fact);

return0;
}
```

This program calculates the factorial of a given number using a for loop.

Infinite Loop

```
#include <stdio.h>

int main() {
    for(;;) {
        printf("Infinite loop\n");
    }
    return 0;
}
```

This program is a straightforward illustration of an endless loop in C, which is frequently utilized in systems that need to run continuously. However, it must be handled cautiously to prevent unexpected program hangs.

Description of Pre-increment:

The pre-increment operator (**++i**) increases the value of a variable by 1 **before** it is used in an expression. The term "pre-increment" is used because the increment operation takes place prior to the evaluation or assignment of the variable's value.

Description of Post-increment:

The post-increment operator (**i++**) increases the value of a variable by 1 **after** it is used in an expression. The term "post-increment" is used because the increment occurs after the evaluation or use of the variable's current value.

Example:

```
#include<stdio.h>
```

```
int main()
{
    int i = 1;

printf("%4d\n", ++i);  /* value of i becomes 2, then printed */
printf("%4d\n", i++);  /* current value 2 is printed, then i becomes 3 */
printf("%4d\n", i);    /* final value of i is 3 */

return0;
}
```

Program to Check Whether a Year is a Leap Year

```
#include<stdio.h>

int main()
{
    int year;

printf("Enter a year: ");
scanf("%d", &year);

    /* A year is a leap year if:
It is divisible by 4 AND not divisible by 100
          OR
       2. It is divisible by 400
    */

if ((year % 4 == 0 && year % 100 != 0) || (year % 400 == 0))
    {
printf("%d is a leap year.\n", year);
    }
else
    {
printf("%d is not a leap year.\n", year);
    }

return0;
}
```

Explanation: This program checks the mathematical conditions required for a leap year. If the year satisfies the leap year rule, it prints that it is a leap year; otherwise, it prints that it is not.

Program to Check Whether a Number is a Palindrome

```
#include<stdio.h>

int main()
```

```
{
    int num, originalNumber, reversedNumber = 0, remainder;

printf("Enter a number: ");
scanf("%d", &num);

originalNumber = num;

    /* Reverse the digits of the number */
while (num != 0)
    {
        remainder = num % 10;
reversedNumber = reversedNumber * 10 + remainder;
num = num / 10;
    }

    /* Compare original and reversed number */
if (originalNumber == reversedNumber)
    {
printf("%d is a palindrome number.\n", originalNumber);
    }
else
    {
printf("%d is not a palindrome number.\n", originalNumber);
    }

return0;
}
```

Explanation: The program reverses the digits of the given number using a while loop. If the reversed number matches the original number, it is a palindrome.

Sample Program Using Do-While Loop

```
#include<stdio.h>

int main()
{
    int number;

    /* The loop executes at least once */
do
    {
printf("Enter a number (0 to stop): ");
scanf("%d", &number);

if (number != 0)
        {
```

```
printf("You entered: %d\n", number);
        }

    } while (number != 0);

printf("Program terminated.\n");

return0;
}
```

Explanation: This program demonstrates the use of a do-while loop. The loop continues to accept input from the user until 0 is entered. Since the condition is checked after execution, the loop runs at least once.

Description: This program illustrates the implementation of a do-while loop to continuously receive numerical input from the user until a 0 is entered. This is a typical illustration demonstrating that a do-while loop executes at least once, irrespective of the circumstance.

Conclusion

Branching statements such as if, if-else, switch, and conditional operators allow a computer to make decisions and execute particular blocks of code contingent upon specified criteria. This enhances adaptability and cognitive capability in programs by enabling them to respond variably to diverse inputs or circumstances. Looping constructs like as for, while, and do-while are employed to iterate a sequence of instructions until a specified condition is fulfilled. This aids in minimizing code redundancy, efficiently managing recurring jobs, and executing operations such as array traversal, calculations, and repeated input acquisition. Branching and looping structures collectively constitute the foundation of structured programming, enabling developers to create logical, efficient, and user-centric systems.

Exercises

These exercises will help you practice and strengthen your understanding of **decision-making** and **looping** constructs like **`if`**, **`switch`**, **`for`**, **`while`**, and **`do-while`**.

Branching (Decision-Making) Exercises:

1. **Even or Odd:** Write a program to check whether a number is even or odd using **`if-else`**.
2. **Largest of Three Numbers:** Input three numbers and use **`if-else-if`** to find the largest.
3. **Grade Calculation:** Take marks (0–100) and print grade:

   a. `A` for 90–100
   b. `B` for 80–89
   c. `C` for 70–79
   d. `F` for below 70

4. **Leap Year Checker:** Use `if` statements to check if a year is a leap year or not.
5. **Simple Calculator:** Use `switch-case` to perform basic arithmetic operations: `+`, `-`, `*`, `/`

Looping Exercises

1. **Print 1 to 10:** Use `for`, `while`, and `do-while` loops separately to print numbers from 1 to 10.
2. **Sum of N Natural Numbers:** Write a program to find the sum of the first N natural numbers.
3. **Factorial Program:** Input a number and print its factorial using a `for` loop.
4. **Multiplication Table:** Print the multiplication table of any number (for example, 5 × 1 to 10).
5. **Reverse a Number:** Use a `while` loop to reverse the digits of an integer (for example, 123 → 321).
6. **Palindrome Number:** Check whether a number is a palindrome using a loop.
7. **Menu-Driven Program (using `do-while`):**
8. Create a simple menu:
   a. Check Even/Odd.
   b. Find Factorial.
   c. Exit.
   d. Loop until the user chooses to exit.

CHAPTER 4
Arrays

Introduction

In the actual world, people commonly put data into groups and collections. The grades of 100 students, the pricing of items in a store, or the average temperatures in a city during a month are all examples of sets of linked values. If we used different variables for each of these values in programming, the program would quickly get too long, hard to manage, and accordingly slow. Arrays are a feature of computer languages that help with this difficulty. An array is a way to organize data components of the same type that are stored in memory locations that are next to each other. An index or subscript identifies each element of an array, making it possible to get to any element in constant time. Arrays are better than single variables because they may hold more than one value under one name. This makes programs more organized and faster. In programming, arrays are the basic building blocks for working with data. They can hold simple values such as integers, characters, and floating-point numbers, as well as more complicated structures like matrices, tables, and multidimensional datasets. In fact, arrays are used to store data internally in higher-level data structures such as stacks, queues, linked lists, trees, and graphs. The study of arrays starts with one-dimensional arrays, which show how items are arranged in a straight line. Next, we shall take a look at the two-dimensional arrays, which are like rows and columns in a spreadsheet, or a math matrix. Multi-dimensional arrays are a more advanced notion that takes the idea to three or more dimensions. They are used in graphics, simulations, and scientific computing. Arrays are useful in many ways, and not just in theory. They are used a lot in algorithms for searching and sorting, image processing, matrix operations, and managing memory. Arrays are one of the most frequent ways to organize data in computer systems, and to learn both basic and advanced programming principles, you need to know how they function.

Structure

In this chapter, we will cover the following topics:

- One-Dimensional Array (1-D Array)

- Two-Dimensional Array (2-D Array)
- Multi-Dimensional Array (M-D Array)
- Array Traversal

Introduction to Arrays

An array is a collection of elements of the same data type stored in contiguous memory locations. It allows you to store multiple values in a single variable instead of declaring separate variables.

Definition

An **array** is a collection of elements of the **same data type** stored in **contiguous memory locations**, and can be accessed using an **index**.

Key Characteristics of Arrays:

- Fixed size (defined at declaration).
- Elements must be of the same data type.
- Indexed (index starts from 0 in C, C++, Java).
- Efficient access to elements using index numbers.

Applications of Arrays:

- **Data Storage**: Storing multiple values under one name.
- **Searching and Sorting**: Used in algorithms like binary search, bubble sort, quick sort, and so on.
- **Matrix Operations**: Addition, subtraction, and multiplication of matrices.
- **Handling Records**: Marks of students, bank transactions, and salaries of employees.
- **Graphs and Trees Representation**: Arrays are used to implement adjacency matrices.
- **Image Processing**: Storing pixel data in 2-D or 3-D arrays.
- **Dynamic Programming**: Arrays are essential for memoization and tabulation.

Accessing Array Element

```
#include <stdio.h>

int main() {
    int arr[5] = {10, 20, 30, 40, 50};
    int i;

    for(i = 0; i < 5; i++) {
```

```
        printf("a[%d] = %d\n", i, arr[i]);
    }
    return 0;
}
```

This C program demonstrates how to **store and access elements of an array using a loop**.

It declares an integer array with five values and uses a for loop to iterate through each element. During each iteration, the program prints both the **index** and the **value** of the array element using the printf function.

The loop starts from index 0 and continues up to 4, ensuring that all elements of the array are accessed sequentially. This approach avoids repetitive codes, and makes it efficient to handle multiple data items.

One-Dimensional Array (1-D Array)

A One-dimensional (1D) array is a fundamental data structure in programming that stores a linear sequence (or list) of elements that all have the same data type. These elements are stored in contiguous memory locations, and are accessed using a single index or subscript.

Declaration

```
data_typearray_name[size];
int arr[5]
```

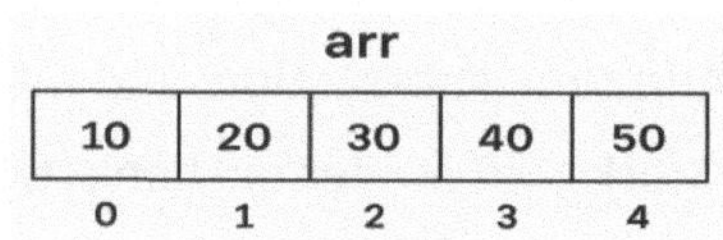

Figure 4.1: *One-Dimensional Array with Index Number*

```
Arr[0]=10, Arr[1]=20, Arr[2]=30, Arr[3]=40 ,Arr[4]=50
```

Sample program of a 1-D array

```
#include <stdio.h>
int main() {
    int arr[10];         // Declare an array of size 10
    int i, sum = 0;
    float avg;

    // Input values into the array
printf("Enter 10 numbers:\n");
for(i = 0; i < 10; i++) {
```

```
        scanf("%d", &arr[i]);
}
    // Calculate sum of array elements
    for(i = 0; i < 10; i++) {
        sum += arr[i];
    }
// Calculate average
    avg = sum / 10.0;

    // Output results
printf("Sum = %d\n", sum);
printf("Average = %.2f\n", avg);

    return 0;
}
```

Explanation:

`int arr [10];` › Declares a 1-D array of size 10.

`for (i = 0; i < 10; i++)`→ Takes the input values from the user.

Another loop calculates the **sum** of all elements.

Average is computed as **`sum / 10.0`**.

Finally, the sum and average are displayed.

Two-Dimensional Array (2-D Array)

An array of arrays is called a two-dimensional array. It lets you store data in rows and columns, like a table or matrix in algebra. A one-dimensional array stores data in a straight line, while a two-dimensional array stores data in a grid.

Syntax:

```
data_typearray_name[rows][columns];
```

```
int matrix [3][3];
```

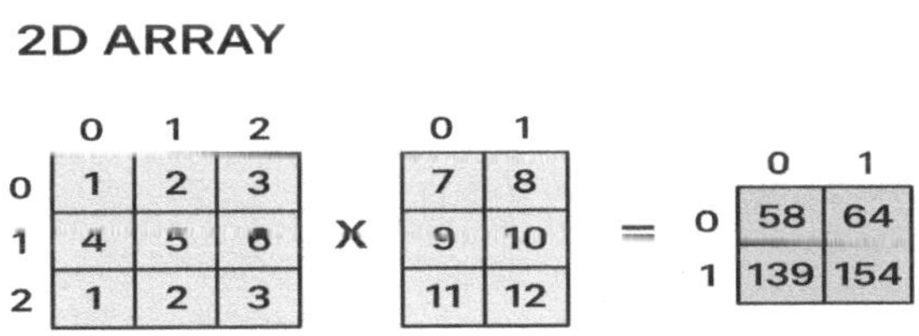

Figure 4.2: *2D Array with Index Number*

Sample Program of a 2D Array (Matrix Multiplication)

```
#include <stdio.h>

int main() {
    int A[10][10], B[10][10], C[10][10];
    int m, n, p, q, i, j, k, sum;

    // Input dimensions of matrices
printf("Enter rows and columns of Matrix A: ");
scanf("%d %d", &m, &n);

printf("Enter rows and columns of Matrix B: ");
scanf("%d %d", &p, &q);

    // Check if multiplication is possible
    if(n != p) {
printf("Matrix multiplication not possible!\n");
        return 0;
    }

    // Input elements of Matrix A
printf("Enter elements of Matrix A:\n");
    for(i = 0; i < m; i++) {
        for(j = 0; j < n; j++) {
scanf("%d", &A[i][j]);
        }
    }

    // Input elements of Matrix B
printf("Enter elements of Matrix B:\n");
    for(i = 0; i < p; i++) {
        for(j = 0; j < q; j++) {
scanf("%d", &B[i][j]);
        }
    }

    // Multiply matrices
    for(i = 0; i < m; i++) {
        for(j = 0; j < q; j++) {
            sum = 0;
            for(k = 0; k < n; k++) {
                sum += A[i][k] * B[k][j];
            }
            C[i][j] = sum;
        }
    }
```

```
    // Print result
printf("Resultant Matrix (A × B):\n");
    for(i = 0; i < m; i++) {
        for(j = 0; j < q; j++) {
printf("%d ", C[i][j]);
        }
printf("\n");
    }

    return 0;
}
```

Explanation:

Matrix A (2×3):

```
1   2   3
4   5   6
```

Matrix B (3×2):

```
7   8
9   10
11  12
```

Step 1: Dimensions.

A is **2×3**, B is **3×2**.

Since n=3 = p=3, multiplication is possible.

Result C will be **2×2**.

Step 2: Calculate each element of C.

(i) **First Row × First Column → C[0][0]**

C[0][0]=(1×7)+(2×9)+(3×11)=7+18+33=58C[0][0] = (1×7) + (2×9) + (3×11) = 7 + 18 + 33 = 58C[0][0]=(1×7)+(2×9)+(3×11)=7+18+33=58

(ii) **First Row × Second Column → C[0][1]**

C[0][1]=(1×8)+(2×10)+(3×12)=8+20+36=64C[0][1] = (1×8) + (2×10) + (3×12) = 8 + 20 + 36 = 64C[0][1]=(1×8)+(2×10)+(3×12)=8+20+36=64

(iii) **Second Row × First Column → C[1][0]**

C[1][0]=(4×7)+(5×9)+(6×11)=28+45+66=139C[1][0] = (4×7) + (5×9) + (6×11) = 28 + 45 + 66 = 139C[1][0]=(4×7)+(5×9)+(6×11)=28+45+66=139

(iv) **Second Row × Second Column → C[1][1]**

C[1][1]=(4×8)+(5×10)+(6×12)=32+50+72=154C[1][1] = (4×8) + (5×10) + (6×12) = 32 + 50 + 72 =154C[1][1]=(4×8)+(5×10)+(6×12)=32+50+72=154

Multi-Dimensional Array (M-D Array)

A **Multi-Dimensional array** is an array that contains more than one dimension of data. It can be visualized as an **array of arrays**, where each element itself may be another array.

- **1-D Array**→ Linear list (like a row).
- **2-D Array**→ Rectangular grid (rows × columns).
- **3-D Array**→ Collection of 2-D arrays (like stacked tables, forming a cube).
- **n-D Array**→ Generalization of arrays with n dimensions.

```
#include <stdio.h>

int main() {
    int arr[2][3][2];  // 3-D array: 2 blocks, 3 rows, 2 columns
    int i, j, k;

    // Input elements
printf("Enter elements of 3-D array (2 blocks × 3 rows × 2 cols):\n");
    for(i = 0; i < 2; i++) {            // Blocks
        for(j = 0; j < 3; j++) {        // Rows
            for(k = 0; k < 2; k++) {  // Columns
printf("arr[%d][%d][%d] = ", i, j, k);
scanf("%d", &arr[i][j][k]);
}
        }
    }

    // Display elements
printf("\n3-D Array Elements:\n");
    for(i = 0; i < 2; i++) {
printf("Block %d:\n", i);
        for(j = 0; j < 3; j++) {
            for(k = 0; k < 2; k++) {
printf("%d ", arr[i][j][k]);
            }
printf("\n");
        }
printf("\n");
    }

    return 0;
}
```

Explanation:

We declare **`arr[2][3][2]`**:

2 blocks → like 2 matrices.

Each block has 3 rows and 2 columns.

Input Loop: Nested loops are used to fill elements at positions **`(i, j, k)`**.

Output Loop: Prints elements block by block, like stacked 2-D tables.

Characteristics:

- Stores homogeneous elements (same data type).
- Elements are stored in adjacent memory regions.
- Accessed via numerous indices, one for each dimension.
- The size of each dimension must be established at the time of declaration.

Array Traversal

Array traversal refers to the act of accessing and processing each element of an array precisely one time. This is typically accomplished by a loop (for, while, or do-while). Traversal enables the execution of actions, including element display, value summation, data searching, or modification.

Array Traversal (1-D Array)

```
#include <stdio.h>
int main() {
    int arr[5] = {1, 2, 3, 4, 5};
    int i;

printf("Array elements are:\n");
    for(i = 0; i < 5; i++) {
printf("%d ", arr[i]);
    }
    return 0;
}
```

Array Traversal (2-D Array)

```
#include <stdio.h>
int main() {
    int matrix[2][3] = {{1, 2, 3}, {4, 5, 6}};
    int i, j;

printf("Matrix elements are:\n");
```

```
    for(i = 0; i < 2; i++) {
        for(j = 0; j < 3; j++) {
printf("%d ", matrix[i][j]);
        }
printf("\n"); // new line for each row
    }
    return 0;
}
```

Program Explanation

```
int matrix[2][3] = {{1, 2, 3}, {4, 5, 6}};
```

Declares and initializes a **2 × 3 array**.

The array looks like:

```
Row 0 → 1   2   3
Row 1 → 4   5   6
```

The nested **for** loops are used for traversal:

Outer loop → controls **rows** (**i**).

Inner loop → controls **columns** (**j**).

```
printf ("%d ", matrix[i][j]);
```

Prints each element of the matrix.

```
printf("\n");
```

After each row is printed, it moves to the next line.

Applications of Traversal:

- Displaying all elements of an array.
- Summing or averaging array values.
- Searching for a particular element.
- Modifying or updating array contents.

Array Reversal using two pointers

```
#include <stdio.h>

int main() {
int arr[] = {1, 2, 3, 4, 5};
int n = 5;

int start = 0, end = n - 1;
while (start < end) {
// swap
```

```
int temp = arr[start];
arr[start] = arr[end];
arr[end] = temp;

start++;
end--;
}

// print reversed array
for (int i = 0; i < n; i++) {
printf("%d ", arr[i]);
}

return 0;
}
```

Array Reversal using recursion

```
#include <stdio.h>

void reverse(int arr[], int start, int end)
{
if (start >= end)
return;

int temp = arr[start];
arr[start] = arr[end];
arr[end] = temp;

reverse(arr, start + 1, end - 1);
}

int main() {
int arr[] = {1, 2, 3, 4, 5};
int n = 5;

reverse(arr, 0, n - 1);

for (int i = 0; i < n; i++) {
printf("%d ", arr[i]);
}

return 0;
}
```

Duplicate number findings using 1D array

```
#include <stdio.h>

int main() {
    int arr[] = {1, 3, 4, 2, 2, 3};
```

```
    int n = 6;

    for (int i = 0; i < n; i++) {
        for (int j = i + 1; j < n; j++) {
            if (arr[i] == arr[j]) {
                printf("Duplicate: %d\n", arr[i]);
                break;
            }
        }
    }
    return 0;
}
```

Array of Pointers

An Array of Pointers is a form of array where each element is a pointer variable instead of a regular data element. The array does not store direct values such as integers, floats, or characters. Instead, it keeps the addresses of variables or data pieces.

This gives us more options for how to work with data because we can use pointers to:

- You may dynamically reference variables, strings, and even functions.
- Handle data of different lengths, notably strings.
- Manage memory that changes.

Declaration:

```
data_type *array_name[size];
int *ptr[5];    // Array of 5 integer pointers
```

Sample program to execute an array of pointers:

```
#include <stdio.h>
int main() {
    int a = 10, b = 20, c = 30;
    int *arr[3];    // Array of integer pointers

arr[0] = &a;
arr[1] = &b;
arr[2] = &c;

"Values using array of pointers:\n");
    for(int i = 0; i < 3; i++) {
printf("%d\n", *arr[i]);    // Dereferencing pointer
    }

    return 0;
}
```

Explanation

arr[0]→ address of a

*arr[0]→ value at that address →10

arr[1]→ address of b

*arr[1]→20

Key Applications of an Array of Pointers:

- Efficient management of strings, such as command-line arguments (**argv**).
- **Malloc()** and **calloc()** are used to allocate memory dynamically.
- Developing data structures that are founded on pointers.
- Function pointer arrays are advantageous in system programming.

Pointer to an Array

Pointers are variables in C programming that contain the addresses of other variables. Pointers are typically employed to reference individual variables or the initial constituent of an array.

Nevertheless, there are instances in which a block-level pointer is required to refer to an entire array. This is referred to as a Pointer to an Array.

Sample program to execute Pointer to an Array

```
#include <stdio.h>

int main() {
    int arr[5] = {10, 20, 30, 40, 50};

    int (*ptr)[5];  // pointer to an array of 5 integers
ptr = &arr;     // store address of whole array

printf("Elements of array using pointer to array:\n");
    for (int i = 0; i < 5; i++) {
printf("%d ", (*ptr)[i]);  // dereference and index
    }

    return 0;
}
```

Aspect	Array of Pointers	Pointer to Array
Definition	A collection of pointers, where each pointer can point to a different variable or array.	A single pointer that stores the address of an entire array as one block.
Declaration	`int *arr[5];` → array of 5 pointers to int	`int (*ptr)[5];` → pointer to an array of 5 integers
Memory Allocation	Each element of the array holds a separate pointer (addresses of variables or arrays).	A single pointer points to the start address of the whole array.
Accessing Elements	If `arr[i]` is a pointer → element = `*arr[i]`	If `ptr` points to array → element = `(*ptr)[i]`
Pointer Arithmetic	`arr+1` moves to the next pointer (size depends on pointer type).	`ptr+1` skips the entire array block (jumps by the size of the whole array).
Usage	Used when you need multiple references to different data (like a list of strings).	Used when handling an array as a single unit (like passing 2D arrays).
Example	`char *names[3] = {"Ram", "Shyam", "Sita"};`	`int (*p)[4]; int a[4]; p = &a;`

Table 4.1: *Difference between an Array of Pointers and a Pointer to an Array*

Conclusion

Arrays are one of the most important and widely used data structures in C programming. They enable programmers to store multiple values of the same data type in a single variable, which simplifies data management and reduces the need for multiple variable declarations. By using indexing, arrays allow easy and fast access to elements, making operations like searching, sorting, and traversal more efficient.

Arrays enable for greater memory efficiency and performance by storing elements in contiguous memory areas. They are particularly helpful in applications like data processing, algorithm construction, and mathematical calculations that require managing substantial volumes of data.

Arrays do have certain restrictions, though. Their size cannot be altered during runtime and must be predetermined, which could result in memory waste or inadequate storage. Furthermore, only components of the same data type can be stored in arrays.

In conclusion, arrays are a basic idea and building block for more complex data structures in programming because they offer a straightforward, effective, and systematic method of storing and manipulating data.

Questions

1. Define an array in C.
2. Write the syntax of declaring a one-dimensional array.
3. What is the difference between int `arr[5];` and `int *arr;`?
4. If `arr[0]` is at address 1000 and each element takes 4 bytes, what is the address of `arr[3]`?
5. State any two advantages of using arrays.
6. Differentiate between an **array of pointers** and a **pointer to an array**.
7. Write a program to find the largest element in a one-dimensional array.
8. Explain 2D arrays with a suitable example and diagram.
9. How can you initialize a 2D array in C? Give an example.
10. Write a program to read 10 integers into an array and print them in reverse order.
11. Write a C program to add two 2D matrices of size 3x3.
12. Explain with a program how to pass an array to a function in C.
13. Differentiate between **1D**, **2D**, and **multi-dimensional arrays** with examples.
14. Describe the relation between **arrays and pointers** with examples.
15. Write a program to sort an array of integers in ascending order.
16. Write a program to search for an element in an array using **linear search**.
17. Write a program to calculate the sum of the diagonal elements of a 2D array.
18. Write a program using a pointer-to-array to access elements of a 1D array.
19. Write a program using an array of pointers to store and print a list of strings.

CHAPTER 5
Algorithms

Introduction

An algorithm refers to a detailed sequence of steps or a clearly defined collection of instructions, which aims at addressing a particular issue, or executing a calculation. Algorithms serve as the cornerstone of computer science and programming. Every operation a computer carries out—whether it is sorting numbers, locating data, encrypting information, or processing images—is fundamentally based on them.

The term originates from the Persian mathematician Al-Khwarizmi (9th century), whose contributions introduced organized methods for problem-solving.

Structure

In this chapter, we will cover the following topics:

- Characteristics of a Good Algorithm
- Representations of Algorithms
- Classification of Algorithms
- Common Algorithms with Examples
- Complexity of Algorithms

Characteristics of a Good Algorithm

A good algorithm should have the following properties:

- **Input**: Clearly defined inputs are required.
- **Output**: Produces at least one output.
- **Definiteness**: Each step must be unambiguous.
- **Finiteness**: Must terminate after a finite number of steps.
- **Correctness**: Must produce correct results for valid inputs.
- **Efficiency**: Should solve problems using minimal resources (time and space).

Representations of Algorithms

Algorithms can be represented in several forms:

- **Natural Language:** Writing the steps in simple English.

  Example: To find the sum of two numbers:

  1. Take two numbers.
  2. Add them.
  3. Print the result.

- **Pseudocode:** A structured, language-independent way of writing an algorithm.

  Algorithm Add Numbers (a, b)

  Step 1: Input a, b

  Step 2: sum ← a + b

  Step 3: Print sum

  End Algorithm

- **Iterative Method:** An iterative method uses loops (such as **`for`**, **`while`**, and **`do-while`**) to repeatedly execute a block of code until a specific condition is met, or a predefined number of iterations has been reached. The **`for`** loop is particularly suited for iteration when the number of repetitions is known in advance.

```
Algorithm Factorial Iterative(n)
  Step 1: Initialize fact ← 1
  Step 2: For i ← 1 to n do
             fact ← fact * i
  Step 3: Print fact
End Algorithm
```

- **Recursive Method:** A recursive method for a loop is a programming technique where a function repeatedly calls itself to perform the same task that a standard iterative loop (**`for`**, **`while`**) would otherwise handle.

```
Algorithm Factorial_Recursive(n)
  Step 1: If n = 0 or n = 1 then
              return 1
  Step 2: Else
              return n * Factorial_Recursive(n-1)
End Algorithm
```

Classification of Algorithms

- **Brute Force Algorithms**
    - Try all possible solutions.
    - **Example:** Checking every key combination in password cracking.
- **Divide and Conquer**
    - Break the problem into smaller sub-problems; solve them individually; and, then accordingly combine.
    - **Example:** Merge Sort, Quick Sort, Binary Search.
- **Greedy Algorithms**
    - Take the best choice at each step.
    - **Example:** Huffman Coding, Activity Selection.
- **Dynamic Programming**
    - Solves problems with overlapping sub-problems using stored results.
    - **Example:** Fibonacci Sequence, Shortest Paths.
- **Backtracking**
    - Try possible solutions and abandon when wrong.
    - **Example:** N-Queens Problem, Sudoku Solver.
- **Randomized Algorithms**
    - Use randomness to improve efficiency.
    - **Example:** Randomized Quick Sort.

Common Algorithms with Examples

Common algorithms are sets of step-by-step instructions for solving a problem. They can be categorized into several types, including sorting, searching, graph, and machine learning algorithms, each used for specific tasks with varying efficiencies.

Searching Algorithms

Searching algorithms are fundamental concepts in computer science used to locate a specific item within a collection of data. These systematic procedures are pivotal for efficient data retrieval in various applications, from database systems and file searches to complex AI and navigation systems.

Linear Search

Linear Search is a simple, sequential method that checks each element one by one, and works on both sorted and unsorted data.

- Start at the beginning, check each element until found.
- Time Complexity: O(n).

```
Algorithm Linear Search (arr, n, key)
  Step 1: For i ← 0 to n-1 do
             If arr[i] = key then
                Print "Element found at position", i
                Exit
  Step 2: If key not found then
             Print "Element not found"
End Algorithm
```

Algorithm (Step-by-Step)

Input: Array A of size n, element x to search
Output: Index of x if found, otherwise -1

1. Set i = 0
2. Repeat while i< n:
   - If A[i] == x, return i (element found)
   - Else, increment i
3. If i = n, return -1 (element not found)

Array: [4, 2, 9, 1, 5]
Search for 9:

1. Check A[0] = 4 → Not 9
2. Check A[1] = 2 → Not 9
3. Check A[2] = 9 → Found

Output: Index = 2

Binary Search

Binary Search is much more efficient for large, *sorted* datasets, as it repeatedly divides the search interval in half to quickly narrow down the location of the target element.

```
Binary Search(A, n, x)
    low = 0
    high = n - 1

    while low <= high do
```

```
        mid = (low + high) / 2
        if A[mid] == x then
            return mid
        else if A[mid] < x then
            low = mid + 1
        else
            high = mid - 1
    return -1
```

Flowchart

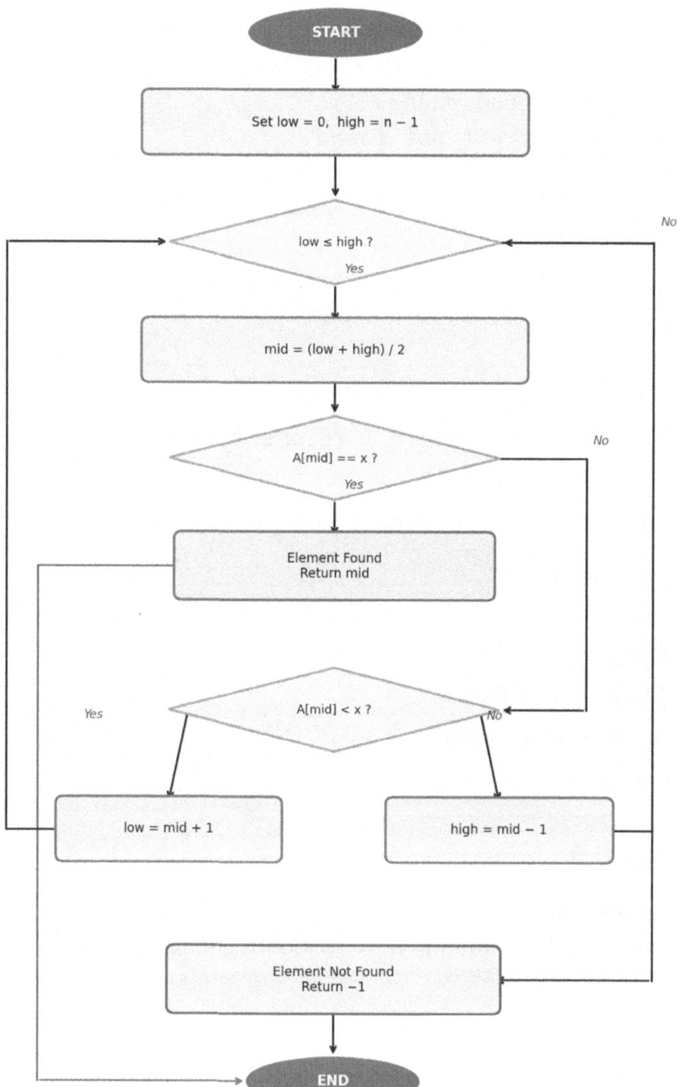

Figure 5.1: *Binary Search Flowchart*

Steps in the flowchart:

1. `Start`
2. `Set low = 0, high = n-1`
3. `Check low ≤ high`
   - `No → Element not found → End`
4. `Calculate mid = (low + high)/2`
5. `Check A[mid] == x`
   - `Yes → Element found → End`
   - `No → Check A[mid] < x`
     - `Yes → low = mid + 1 → Go to step 3`
     - `No → high = mid - 1 → Go to step 3`

```
Array: [2, 5, 8, 12, 16, 23, 38]
Search for 16:
   1. low = 0, high = 6, mid = 3 → A[3] = 12
   2. 12 < 16 → low = mid + 1 = 4
   3. mid = (4+6)/2 = 5 → A[5] = 23
   4. 23 > 16 → high = mid - 1 = 4
   5. mid = (4+4)/2 = 4 → A[4] = 16 → Found
Output: Index = 4
```

Binary Search works on the principle of **divide and conquer**. Instead of checking elements one by one, it repeatedly divides the search space into two halves. First, the middle element of the array is compared with the target value. If the target matches the middle element, the search is successful. If the target is smaller than the middle element, the search continues in the left half of the array; if it is larger, the search continues in the right half. This process is repeated until the element is found, or the search space becomes empty.

Sorting Algorithms

A sorting algorithm is a method for arranging elements of a list in a specific order, such as numerical or lexicographical, ascending or descending. They are fundamental in computer science, used for organizing data to enable more efficient searching and data analysis.

Bubble Sort

Bubble sort is one of the fundamental forms of sorting in programming. Bubble sort algorithms move through a sequence of data (typically integers) and rearrange them into ascending or descending order one number at a time. To do this, the algorithm compares number X to the adjacent number Y.

Algorithm (Step-by-Step)

Input: Array A of size n
Output: Sorted array in ascending order

1. Repeat i from 0 to n-2:
    - Repeat j from 0 to n-i-2:
        - If A[j] > A[j+1], swap A[j] and A[j+1]
2. Continue until no swaps are required.

Flowchart

Steps in the flowchart:

1. Start
2. Set i = 0
3. Set j = 0
4. Compare A[j] and A[j+1]
    - If A[j] > A[j+1] → Swap → Increment j
    - Else → Increment j
5. If j < n-i-1 → Go to step 4
6. Increment i
7. If i< n-1 → Go to step 3
8. End

Example

Array: [5, 2, 9, 1, 5]

Pass 1: [2, 5, 1, 5, 9] → 9 bubbled to the end
Pass 2: [2, 1, 5, 5, 9]
Pass 3: [1, 2, 5, 5, 9]
Pass 4: [1, 2, 5, 5, 9] → Already sorted

Output: [1, 2, 5, 5, 9]

Complexity

In computer science, complexity signifies the number of resources an algorithm needs to address a particular problem. It indicates the efficiency of an algorithm.

Complexity is of two types:

- **Time Complexity:** How much time an algorithm takes to run?
- **Space Complexity:** How much memory an algorithm uses?

Time Complexity quantifies the increase in execution time of an algorithm as the input size grows, usually represented as n.

Common Cases:

- **Best Case:** The scenario where the algorithm runs the fastest.
- **Worst Case:** The scenario where the algorithm runs the slowest.
- **Average Case:** The expected running time for a typical input.

Example: Linear Search

Suppose, we search for an element in an array of size n.

Case	Time Complexity
Best Case	O(1)
Worst Case	O(n)
Average Case	O(n/2) ≈ O(n)

Table 5.1: *Best Case and Time Complexity*

The space complexity of an algorithm refers to the quantity of memory required for execution as a function of the input size. It encompasses all memory utilized during execution:

- Input data storage
- Auxiliary storage (temporary variables)
- Function call stack (in recursive algorithms)

Notation	Name	Description	Example Algorithm
O(1)	Constant	Runs in fixed time regardless of input size.	Array index access
O(log n)	Logarithmic	Halves the problem at each step.	Binary Search
O(n)	Linear	Time grows proportionally with input size.	Linear Search
$O(n^2)$	Quadratic	Time grows as the square of input size.	Bubble Sort, Selection Sort

Table 5.2: *Comparison of Common Algorithm Complexities*

Asymptotic Notation

Asymptotic Notation is a mathematical tool used to show how the running time or space needed by an algorithm changes as the input amount (n) gets bigger. Focusing on the growth rate of algorithms helps when we are looking at them without considering machine-specific factors.

Types of Asymptotic Notation:

- Big-O Notation (O)
- Omega Notation (Ω)
- Theta Notation (Θ)

Big-O Notation (O)

Big O notation characterizes an algorithm's efficiency and scalability by establishing an upper limit on its time or space complexity as the input size (n) increases. It emphasizes the worst-case scenario and the principal term, disregarding constants and lower-order terms to evaluate the fundamental growth rates of various algorithms. This assists developers in identifying the most efficient algorithm by comprehending how its resource consumption scales with increased input sizes.

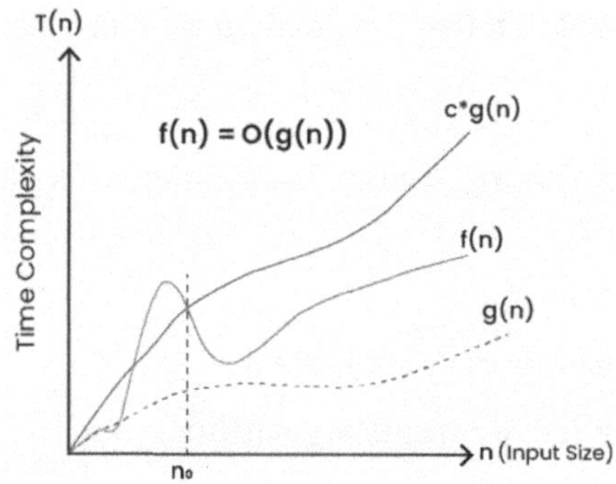

Figure 5.2: *BIG-O Notation*

For two functions `f(n)` and `g(n)`, we define `f(n)` as `O(g(n))` if there exist constants `c > 0` and `n0 ≥ 0` such that `f(n) ≤ c*g(n)` for every `n ≥ n0`. Formally, `f(n)` is `O(g(n))` if there exist constants `c` and `n0` such that `f(n)` does not exceed `c*g(n)` for any `n ≥ n0`.

Omega Notation (Ω)

Omega Notation (Ω) in algorithm analysis, establishes a lower bound on a function's growth rate, usually denoting the best-case temporal complexity of an algorithm.

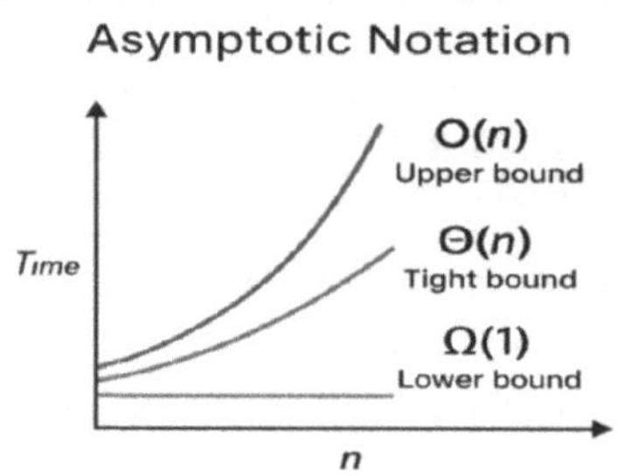

Figure 5.3: *Asymptotic Notation*

- Facilitates comprehension of the algorithm's minimal resource requirements.
- Complements Big-O, which demonstrates the worst-case scenario.
- In the best-case scenario, this is beneficial for performance guarantees.

Theta notation(Θ)

Theta (Θ) notation establishes a precise bound on an algorithm's performance by specifying both its lower and upper limits. It specifies that the algorithm's execution time increases at the same rate as another function, '**g(n)**', for a given input size '**n**'. Informally, **f(n)** is **Θ(g(n))** if there are positive constants c□, c□, and n□ such that $c_1 * g(n) \le f(n) \le c_2 * g(n)$ for all $n \ge n_0$. This implies that c is both the closest lower bound (Omega) and the closest upper bound (Big O) of **f(n)**.

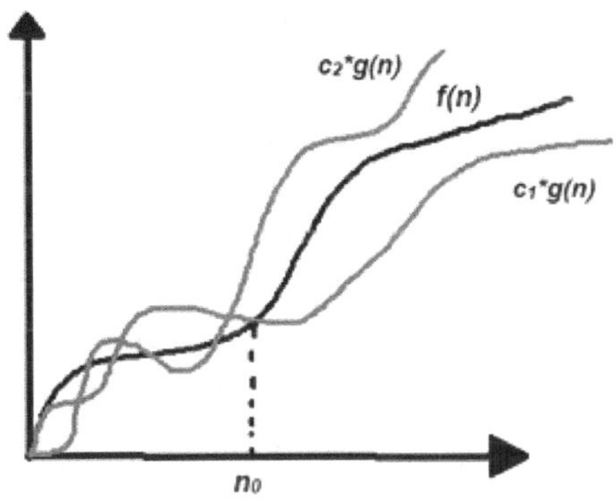

Figure 5.4: *Theta Notation*

The Big - Theta(Θ) notation represents a tight bound on an algorithm's growth rate and specifies asymptotic bounds (both upper and lower) for a function **f(n)**. It does not represent average case complexity, rather, it means the algorithm's running time grows at exactly the rate of **g(n)**. The tight bound of any program can be determined by following these methods:

- Divide the program into smaller segments.
- Determine the quantity and variety of inputs and determine the number of operations required to execute them. Ensure that the input cases are distributed equitably.
- Divide the sum of all the calculated values by the total number of inputs. Let g(n) be the function of n that is obtained after the constants are removed. In Θ notation, it is represented as Θ(g(n)).

Dynamic Programming

Dynamic Programming (DP) is a powerful design technique used to solve optimization problems efficiently. It was introduced by Richard Bellman in the 1950s. DP is closely related to the divide and conquer approach, where a problem is broken down into smaller sub-problems that can be solved individually.

However, DP differs from divide and conquer in a key way: instead of solving the same sub-problems repeatedly through recursion, it solves each sub-problem only once and stores the results in a table. These stored solutions are then reused whenever needed, reducing redundant computations. The final solution to the original problem is obtained by combining the solutions of these sub-problems.

The Steps for Dynamic Programming Technique are:

1. **Dividing the problem into sub-problems:** The main problem is divided into smaller subproblems. The solution of the main problem is expressed in terms of the solution for the smaller sub-problems.
2. **Storing the sub-solutions in a table:** The solution for each sub-problem is stored in a table so that it can be referred many times whenever required.
3. **Bottom-up computation**: Dynamic Programming (DP) begins by solving the **smallest instances** of a problem and gradually builds up solutions to larger subproblems until the final solution to the original problem is obtained.This technique is especially useful when a problem can be seen as a **sequence of decisions**. The goal is to determine an **optimal sequence of decisions**, where each step contributes to the best overall solution. In DP, this is achieved using the **principle of optimality**, introduced by Richard Bellman. According to this principle, regardless of the initial state and decision, the remaining decisions must form an optimal solution for the resulting sub-problem.

A key difference between **greedy algorithms** and **dynamic programming** lies in how decisions are made:

- In the greedy approach, only **one decision path** is followed by choosing the best option at each step.
- In contrast, dynamic programming may explore **multiple decision sequences** and store intermediate results to ensure correctness.

As a result, dynamic programming **guarantees an optimal solution**, whereas greedy algorithms do not always provide such a guarantee.

Matrix Chain Multiplication

Let, we have three matrices A1, A2 and A3, with order (10 x 100), (100 x 5) and (5 x 50) respectively.

Then the three matrices can be multiplied in two ways.

(i) First, multiplying A2 and A3, then multiplying A1 with the resultant matrix i.e. A1(A2 A3).

(ii) First, multiplying A1 and A2, and then multiplying the resultant matrix with A3 i.e. (A1A2) A3.

The number of scalar multiplications required in case 1 is 100 * 5 * 50 + 10 * 100 * 50 = 25000 + 50,000= 75,000 and the number of scalar multiplications required in case 2 is 10 * 100 * 5 + 10 * 5 * 50 = 5000+ 2500 = 7500

To find the best possible way to calculate the product, we could simply parenthesize the expression in every possible fashion and count each time how many scalar multiplications are required. Thus the matrix chain multiplication problem can be stated as "find the optimal parenthesisation of a chain of matrices to be multiplied such that the number of scalar multiplications is minimized".

Conclusion

Algorithms constitute the fundamental basis for problem-solving in computer science. They offer a systematic, methodical approach to resolve issues promptly and effectively. An effective algorithm is finite, definite, and efficient, guaranteeing accurate outputs in minimal time and optimal resource utilization. Comprehending algorithms, their design methodologies, and analytical tools such as time and space complexity is essential for creating efficient programs and software applications. Mastery of algorithms not only improves coding skills, but also strengthens logical thinking, planning, and problem-solving abilities, which are essential for both academic and professional success in computing. Learning algorithms enable individuals to methodically and efficiently address both simple and complicated computing challenges.

Questions

Basic / Conceptual Questions

1. Define an algorithm and explain its characteristics.
2. What is the difference between an algorithm and a program?
3. Explain the importance of algorithms in problem-solving.
4. List the steps involved in designing an algorithm.
5. What is pseudocode? How is it different from a flowchart?

Algorithm Design Techniques

6. Explain the **divide and conquer** technique with an example.
7. What is the **greedy method** in algorithms? Give one example.
8. Describe **dynamic programming** and how it differs from divide and conquer.
9. Explain **backtracking** with an example.
10. What is **recursion**? Write an example of a recursive algorithm.

Searching and Sorting Algorithms

11. Write an algorithm for **linear search**.
12. Write an algorithm for **binary search**.
13. Explain the **bubble sort** algorithm with an example.
14. Explain the **selection sort** algorithm.
15. Compare **bubble sort** and **insertion sort** in terms of complexity.

Flowchart and Pseudocode

16. Draw a **flowchart** to check if a number is even or odd.
17. Convert a given flowchart into **pseudocode**.
18. Draw a flowchart to find the **largest number in an array**.
19. Write a pseudocode to **calculate the factorial** of a number.
20. Explain the difference between a flowchart and an algorithm.

Complexity Analysis

21. Define **time complexity** and **space complexity**.
22. Explain **best case, worst case, and average case** complexity with examples.
23. Define **Big O, Omega, and Theta notation**.
24. Find the time complexity of **linear search**, **binary search**, and **bubble sort**.
25. Discuss why algorithm efficiency is important for large datasets.

Advanced / Problem-Solving Questions

26. Give an example where a **greedy algorithm fails** to give the optimal solution.
27. Explain the **importance of recursion** and its disadvantages.
28. What is an **NP-complete problem**? Give an example.
29. Compare **iterative and recursive algorithms**.
30. Explain the concept of **asymptotic analysis** with an example.

Programming/Application Questions

31. Write an algorithm to **find the GCD of two numbers**.
32. Write an algorithm to **check if a number is a prime number or not**.
33. Write an algorithm to **generate the Fibonacci sequence** up to N terms.
34. Write an algorithm to **merge two sorted arrays** into a single sorted array.
35. Write an algorithm to **find the second-largest element** in an array.

CHAPTER 6
C Function

Introduction

A function in programming is a block of code that can run by itself, and is meant to do one thing. Functions let programmers gather instructions that are similar and use them again instead of writing the same code again. A function normally takes some input, called parameters, processes it, and then gives back an output, called the return value. This makes programs easier to read, modular, and reusable.

A function in programming is a piece of code that is meant to do a certain job. It puts a group of instructions together so that they can be run whenever the function is invoked. We can write the same code once and put it in a function so that we can use it again. Functions help organize programs, make them more modular, and make them easier to understand. They also let programmers break a big problem down into smaller ones, which speeds up the process of writing, fixing, and keeping programs up to date.

Structure

In this chapter, we will cover the following topics:

- Types of Functions
- Formal Parameters and Actual Parameters
- Passing Parameters to Functions or Types of Argument Passing
- Storage Classes

Types of Functions

C functions can be classified into **two** types:

- Library functions /pre-defined functions /standard functions /built-in functions
- User-defined functions

Library Functions

These functions are defined in the **library of C compiler,** which are used frequently in the C program. These functions are written by the designers of the C compiler. C supports many built-in functions such as:

- Mathematical functions (Example: **`pow (x, y)`**: computes **xy).**
- String manipulation functions (Example: **`sqrt(x)`**: computes square root of **`x`**).
- Input and output functions (Example: **`printf ()`**: used to print the data on the screen).
- Memory management functions (**`scanf ()`**: used to read the data from the keyboard).

User-Defined Functions

User-Defined Functions (UDFs) are the functions that the programmer or the user writes to execute certain tasks. The user can create their own functions to do a certain job. Functions that the user makes are called user-defined functions.

Elements of User-Defined Function

The three elements of user-defined function structure are:

- Function definition
- Function declaration
- Function call

Function Definition

A program module written to achieve a specific task is called a function definition.

Each function definition consists of two parts:

- Function header
- Function body

Function Definition Syntax	Function Definition Example

Datatype function name(parameters)
{
`declaration part;`
`executable part;`
`return statement;`
}
	`void add ()`
	`{`
	`int sum, a,b;`
	`printf ("enter a and b\n");`
	`scanf("%d%d",&a,&b);`
	`sum=a+b;`
	`printf ("sum is %d", sum);`
	`}`

Table 6.1: *Function Definition and Example*

Function Declaration

Function declaration or function prototype is the process of saying what a function does before using it. Function declaration has the function's data type, name, and a list of parameters that ends with a semicolon.

Function Declaration Syntax

```
Data type function name (type p1, type p2, ………type pn);
```

Example

```
int add (int a, int b);
void add (int a, int b);
```

Function Call

The process of calling a function to accomplish a particular action is referred to as a function call. A function call is defined as the name of the function followed by a semicolon. A function call is the act of invoking a function at the appropriate location in the program to accomplish a specific action.

```
void main ()
{
    Add ( ); // function call without parameter
}
```

Formal Parameters and Actual Parameters

The variables defined in the function header of the function definition are called formal parameters. All the variables should be separately declared, and each declaration must be separated by commas. The formal parameters receive the data from actual parameters.

The variables that are used when a function is invoked in a function call are called actual parameters. Using actual parameters, the data can be transferred from the calling function to the called function. The corresponding formal parameters in the function definition receive them.

The actual parameters and formal parameters must match in number and type of data.

Actual Parameters	Formal Parameters
Actual parameters are also called **argument list.** Ex: `add(m,n)`	Formal parameters are also called **dummy parameters.** **Ex:** `int add (int a, int b)`
The variables used in a function call are called actual parameters.	The variables defined in the function header are called formal parameters.

Actual Parameters	Formal Parameters

Actual parameters are used in calling a function when a function is called or invoked.
Ex: `add (m, n)`
Here, m and n are called actual parameters.
	Formal parameters are used in the function header of a called function.
	Example:
	`int add (int a, int b)`
	`{ ..........`
	`}`
	Here, a and b are called formal parameters.

Actual parameters send data to the formal parameters.	Formal parameters receive data from the actual parameters.

Table 6.2: *Actual Parameters and Formal Parameters*

Categories of Functions:

- Function with no parameters and no return values.
- Function with no parameters and return values.
- Function with parameters and no return values.
- Function with parameters and return values.

<table>
<tr><th>Calling Function</th><th>Called Function</th></tr>
<tr><td><pre>/*program to find the sum of two
numbers using a function*/
#include<stdio.h> void add ();
void main ()
{
add ();
}</pre></td><td><pre>void add ()
{
int sum;
printf ("enter a and b values\n");
scanf ("%d%d", &a,&b);
sum=a +b;
printf ("\n the sum is %d", sum);
return;
}</pre></td></tr>
<tr><td colspan="2">The called function is unable to receive any values, as no data is transmitted from the calling function to the called function in this category. The user-defined function add () does not receive any arguments in the example. As a result, the function header does not explicitly define any parameters. As the control is transmitted from the calling function to the called function, the values of a and b are read, combined, and the resulting value is displayed on the monitor. Control is transmitted from the called function/add to the calling function/main when the return statement is executed.</td></tr>
</table>

Table 6.3: *Function with no parameters and no return values (void function without parameter)*

At the beginning, the program starts execution from the **main()** function. It first prints "**Calling function**", indicating that a function is about to be called. Then, the function is invoked, and control shifts to it. Inside the function, the statement "**Called function**" is printed, showing that the function is executing. Once the function completes its task, control returns to the **main()** function, and the program either continues with the remaining statements or terminates.

Calling function	Called function
/*program to find the sum of two	void add (int a, int b)
numbers using a function*/	{
#include<stdio.h> void add (int m,	int sum;
int n);	sum = a + b;
void main ()	printf ("sum is: %d", sum);
{	return;
int m, n;	}
printf ("enter values for m and n:");	
scanf ("%d %d",&m,&n);	
add(m,n);	
}	

Table 6.4: *Function with parameters and no return values (void function with parameter)*

Data is transferred from the calling function to the summoned function using parameters in this category. However, there is no data transmission from the called function to the calling function. The values of the actual parameters m and n are transferred to the formal parameters a and b. The sum of the values of a and b is displayed on the screen in the function that is invoked.

Calling Function	Called Function
/*program to find the sum of two	int add () /* function header */
numbers using a function*/	{
#include<stdio.h> int add ();	int a, b, sum;
void main ()	printf ("enter values for a and b:");
{	scanf ("%d %d", &a, &b);
int result; result=add ();	sum= a + b;
printf ("sum is: %d", result);	return sum;
}	}

Table 6.5: *Function with no parameters and with return values*

Data transfer from the called function to the calling function occurs in this category, but not from the calling function to the called function. The function add() does not receive any input. Therefore, the function header does not define any parameters.

The calling function receives one value from the called function and assigns it to the variable result when the function returns a value. The invoking function prints the result value.

Calling Function	Called Function

/*program to find the sum of two numbers using a function*/
#include<stdio.h> int add ();
void main ()
{
int result, m, n;
printf ("enter values for m and n:");
scanf ("%d %d", &m, &n);
result=add (m, n);
printf ("sum is: %d", result);
}
	int add (int a, int b) /* function header */
	{
	int sum;
	sum= a + b;
	return sum;
	}

Table 6.6: *Function with parameters and with return values*

Data transfer between the calling and called functions falls under this category. The values from the calling function can be provided to the formal parameters in the called function when the actual parameters are passed. The calling function receives a value from the called function when the add function returns a value. Formal parameters a and b are created by copying the values of actual parameters m and n. After computation, the sum is returned to the calling function and assigned to the variable result.

Passing Parameters to Functions or Types of Argument Passing

The different ways of passing parameters to the function are:

- Pass by value or call by value.
- Pass by address or call by address.

Call by Value

The values of the actual parameters are replicated into the formal parameters in call by value.

Only a copy of the actual parameters is included in the formal parameters. Therefore, the values of the actual parameters remain unchanged even if the formal parameter values of the called function change.

The concept of call by value can be explained by considering the following program.

Example:

```
#include<stdio.h>
void swap (int a, int b);
void main ()
{
int m, n;
printf ("enter values for a and b:");
scanf ("%d %d", &m, &n);
printf ("the values before swapping is m=%d n=%d \n", m, n);
swap (m, n);
printf ("the values after swapping are m=%d n=%d \n", m, n);
}
void swap (int a, int b)
{
int temp;
temp=a;
 a=b;
 b=temp;
}
```

Explanation

We will read the values for variables m and n, assuming we are reading 10 and 20, respectively, as the execution begins with the function main (). Before switching, we will print the values, which will be 10 and 20. The function swap () is used with m=10 and n=20 as the actual parameters.

The values 10 and 20 are assigned to the formal arguments a and b in the function header of the function swap (). The values of a and b are swapped in the swap () function. In the function main (), however, the values of the actual parameters m and n have not been switched.

The called function does not get the change.

Call by Address

In call by address, the addresses of the real parameters are sent when a function is called. The formal parameters must be stated as pointers of the same type as the real parameters in the called function. Formal parameters are created by copying the addresses of actual parameters. It is possible to modify the values of the real parameters by using these addresses. Pass-by addresses are a method of indirectly altering the real parameters by using their addresses.

Example:

```
#include<stdio.h>
void swap (int a, int b);
void main ()
{
int m, n;
printf ("enter values for a and b:");
scanf ("%d %d", &m, &n);
printf ("the values before swapping are m=%d n=%d \n", m, n);
swap (&m, &n);
printf ("the values after swapping are m=%d n=%d \n", m, n);
}
void swap (int*a, int*b)
{
  int temp;
 temp=*a;
*a=*b;
*b=temp;

}
```

Call by Value	Call by Address
When a function is called, the values of the variables are passed	When a function is called, the addresses of variables are passed
The type of formal parameters should be the same as the type of actual parameters	The type of formal parameters should be the same as the type of actual parameters, but they have to be declared as pointers.
Formal parameters contain the values of actual parameters	Formal parameters contain the addresses of actual parameters

Table 6.7: *Difference between call by value and call by reference*

Scope and Lifetime of a Variable

The scope of a variable is defined as the region or boundary of the program in which the variable is visible. There are two types:

- Global scope
- Local scope

Global Scope

Any variable defined in a program's global area is visible from the time of definition until the program's conclusion. This means that variables defined outside of blocks have global scope.

For instance, variables defined before all functions have global scope and are visible throughout the program.

Local Scope

Local scope refers to the variables defined within a block. They only exist from the moment of their proclamation until the block's conclusion. They cannot be seen from the outside of the block.

Life Span of a Variable

A variable's life span is the amount of time it is active while a program is being executed.

Global variables have a lifespan of the program, while local variables have a lifespan of the function for which they are designed.

Storage Classes

There are the following storage classes which can be used in a C Program:

- Global variables
- Local variables
- Static variables
- Register variables

Global Variables

These variables are defined prior to all functions in the program's global area. These variables receive a single allocation of memory, which is initialized to zero. These variables are not only alive and active throughout the program, but also accessible by any function. When a program is finished running, memory is deallocated.

```
#include<stdio.h>
int x; main ()
{
 x=5;
printf ("%d", x);
printf ("x=%d", fun1 ());
printf ("x=%d", fun2());
printf ("x-%d", fun3());
}
```

Local Variables (Automatic Variables)

These variables, also known as automatic variables, are defined inside functions and have a scope that is restricted to the function in which they are declared. One should, however, note that they are not accessible from outside of the function.

```
#include<stdio.h>
 Main ()
{
int m=1000;
func2();
printf ("%d\n", m);
}
func1()
{
int m=10;
printf ("%d\n", m);
}
```

Static Variables

Static variables are those that are declared using the keyword static. It is possible to declare the static variables both inside and outside of the function. Both local and global variables can be found in them. It is also possible to specify static inside a function.

```
Ex: static int a, b;
#include<stdio.h>
Main ()
{
 int I; for (I=1; I<=3; I++)
 Stat ();
 }
Stat ()
{
static int x=0;
x=x+1;
printf ("x=%d\n", x);
 }
```

Output:

```
x=1
x=2
x=3
```

Register Variables

Register variables are any variables declared with the qualifier register. Historically, this told the compiler to keep the variable in a CPU register rather than main memory for faster access. However, with modern compilers, this keyword is largely ignored. Compilers, today can make far better optimization decisions on their own, and will automatically place frequently-used variables in registers when appropriate. The register keyword is considered obsolete in C11 and later standards.

When compared to memory access, register access is substantially faster. For example: register int a;

Storage Class	Scope	Lifetime	Default Value	Memory Location
Global	Entire program	Program duration	0 (zero)	Data segment (BSS)
Local (auto)	Within function	Function duration	Garbage value	Stack
Static	Within block	Program duration	0 (zero)	Data segment
Register	Within function	Function duration	Garbage value	CPU register (if available)

Table 6.8: *Storage Classes: Comparison Summary*

Program 1: A Given Number is an Armstrong Number or Not Using a Function

```
#include<stdio.h>
int amstrong (int);                    ► Function Prototype
void main ()
{
        int n, k;
        printf ("enter the number");
        scanf ("%d", &n);
        k=amstrong(n);                 ► Function Called
        if(k==n)
        {
```

```
        printf ("The number is armstrong number");
    }
        else
        {
                printf ("The number is not armstrong number");
        }
}
int amstrong (int n)  ——————————→  Function Definition
{
        int i, sum=0, r;
        while(n>0)
        {
                r=n%10;
                sum=sum +r*r*r;
                n=n/10;
        }
        return (sum);
}
```

Output:

```
Enter the number 153
The number is armstrong number
```

Program 2: A Given Number is a Palindrome or Not Using a Function

```
#include<stdio.h>
int palindrome(int);  ——————————→  Function Prototype
void main ()
{
        int n, f=1, k;
        printf ("enter the number");
        scanf ("%d", &n);
        k=palindrome(n);  ——————————→  Function Called
if(k==n)
        {
        printf ("The number is palindrome number");
    }
        else
        {
                printf ("The number is not palindrome number");
```

```
        }
}
int palindrome (int n)
{
        int i, sum=0, r;
        while(n>0)
        {
                r=n%10;
                sum=sum*10+r;
                n=n/10;
        }
        return (sum);
}
```

Function Definition

Output:

```
enter the number 121
The n1umber is palindrome number
```

Conclusion

In C, functions are the fundamental units of modular and structured programming. They enable a programmer to divide a big, complicated program into more manageable, logical chunks that are simpler to create, test, and update. Code becomes more efficient, reusable, and structured when functions are used. Writing clear and efficient programs requires knowing how to declare, define, and call functions, as well as the idea of parameter passing (call by value and call by reference). In conclusion, functions are one of the most potent aspects of the C programming language, since they improve readability, cut down on redundancy, and encourage better program design.

Multiple Choice Questions

1. A function that calls itself is known as:
    a. Inline function
    b. Recursive function
    c. Nested function
    d. None of these
2. Which keyword is used to return a value from a function?
    a. Return
    b. Void

   c. Exit
   d. break
3. In C, if a function does not return any value, its return type is:
   a. Int
   b. Float
   c. Void
   d. None
4. The variables declared inside a function are:
   a. Global variables
   b. Local variables
   c. Static variables
   d. None
5. Which of the following is a standard library function?
   a. `add()`
   b. `printf()`
   c. `factorial()`
   d. `display()`

Questions

Short Answer Questions

1. What is a function in C?
2. Define user-defined and library functions with examples.
3. What are the advantages of using functions in C?
4. Differentiate between a function declaration and a function definition.
5. What is a function prototype? Why is it important?
6. What is the difference between actual parameters and formal parameters?
7. Explain “call by value” and “call by reference” with examples.
8. What is recursion? Give an example.
9. What is the difference between local and global variables?
10. What is the purpose of the return statement in a function?

Conceptual / Descriptive Questions

1. Explain the structure of a function in C with syntax and an example.
2. Describe the various types of user-defined functions with examples.
3. Write the advantages and disadvantages of using recursive functions.
4. Explain the difference between void functions and functions with return types.
5. Describe how arguments are passed to a function.
6. Discuss the scope and lifetime of variables used in a function.
7. Explain the difference between inline functions and normal functions.
8. Illustrate how modular programming is achieved using functions.

Program-Based Questions

1. Write a program to find the sum of two numbers using a function.
2. Write a function to check whether a number is even or odd.
3. Write a program to calculate the factorial using a **recursive function**.
4. Write a program to find the greatest of three numbers using a function with arguments and a return value.
5. Write a function to check whether a number is a prime number or not.
6. Write a program to reverse a number using a function.
7. Write a program to find the sum of the digits of a number using a user-defined function.
8. Write a function that swaps two numbers using **call by reference**.
9. Write a recursive function to generate the Fibonacci series.
10. Write a program to compute the power of a number using a function.

CHAPTER 7
C Recursion

Introduction

Recursion is one of the most powerful and elegant techniques in programming. It is a process in which a **function calls itself** to solve a smaller instance of the same problem. This approach allows programmers to solve complex problems by breaking them down into simpler subproblems. In real life, recursion can be compared to looking at two mirrors facing each other — they create an image that repeats itself endlessly. Similarly, in programming, a recursive function continues calling itself until a specific stopping condition (called the **base case**) is met. Recursion is an implementation technique in which a function solves a problem by calling itself on smaller inputs. While some recursive algorithms employ a divide-and-conquer strategy (such as Merge Sort), recursion itself is broader — for example, computing a factorial is purely recursive but is not divide-and-conquer. To make the primary problem easier to solve directly, it breaks it down into smaller subproblems of the same type. The call stack is where all a function's state information, including its variables and return address, is saved when the function calls itself. After the initialization of the base case, the stored calls begin to return values sequentially.

Structure

In this chapter, we will cover the following topics:

- Stack Frame Explanation
- Types of Functions
- Quicksort Using Recursion
- Power of a Number Using Recursion

Stack Frame Explanation

Every time a recursive function calls itself, the runtime creates a new stack frame on the call stack. Each frame stores the function's local variables, parameters, and return address. As recursion deepens, frames accumulate; once the base case is reached, frames are popped one by one and return values propagate back up.

Example:

factorial(3) call stack growth and unwind:

```
factorial(3)  calls  factorial(2)
factorial(2)  calls  factorial(1)
factorial(1)  calls  factorial(0)  -> returns 1
factorial(1)  <- returns 1*1 = 1
factorial(2)  <- returns 2*1 = 2
factorial(3)  <- returns 3*2 = 6
```

Each level above is one stack frame. Without a reachable base case, frames keep stacking until the program runs out of stack memory, causing a stack overflow.

Types of Functions

C functions can be classified into **two** types:

- Direct recursion (An internal function call is a direct method call to the function itself.)
- Indirect recursion (A function starts a loop by calling another function, which in turn calls the original function.)
- Tail recursion
- Head recursion
- No Tail/ Head recursion
- Linear recursion
- Tree recursion

Direct Recursion

Direct recursion allows a function to call itself inside its own definition. This recursion type in C is very common and easy to understand. As the recursion progresses, the issue size often reduces until the base case is met, at which point the recursion ends.

```
#include <stdio.h>
void directRecursion (int n)
{
if (n > 0)
   {
printf ("%d ", n);
directRecursion (n - 1); // Recursive call
```

```
    }
}
int main ()
{
int num = 5;
printf ("Direct Recursion: ");
directRecursion (num);
return 0;
}
```

Direct recursion is demonstrated in this C code by calling the **directRecursion** function with decreasing '**n**' values until '**n**' = 0. The output is "Direct Recursion: 5 4 3 2 1," which lists the values of n from 5 to 2 in decreasing order.

Indirect Recursion

Indirect recursion occurs when at least two functions call each other in a cycle. These functions work together to resolve an issue by passing control between themselves until a termination condition is met. Despite its rarity, this recursion type is useful in some situations.

```
#include <stdio.h>
void functionB(int n);
void functionA(int n)
 {
if (n > 0) {
printf ("%d ", n);
functionB(n - 1); // Indirect recursive call
 }
}
void functionB(int n) {
 if (n > 0) {
printf ("%d ", n);
functionA(n / 2); // Indirect recursive call
 }
}
int main () {
 int num = 5;
printf ("Indirect Recursion: ");
functionA(num);
 return 0;
}
```

Tail Recursion

There will be no expression or operation waiting to be executed in the function once the recursive call is made via this sort of recursion. Use the following example to better grasp this type of function:

```
int tail_recursion(int n, int accumulator) {
    if n == 0:
        return accumulator
    return tail_recursion(n - 1, n * accumulator);
}
// Output when called as tail_recursion(5, 1): 120
```

No expression or reasoning follows the recursive call in this type of recursion, as you can see. The accumulator has passed the result by the function.

No Tail/Head Recursion

Definition:

If the recursive call is neither the first statement (head), nor the last statement (tail) – that is, it occurs in between other operations, then the function is said to have neither head, nor tail recursion.

Example:

```
void example (int n) {
    if (n == 0)
        return;
printf("%d ", n);    // Operation before recursion
    example (n - 1) ;      // Recursive call
printf ("%d ", n);   // Operation after recursion
}
```

Explanation: Here, part of the work is done **before** and part **after** the recursive call. Thus, the function is **neither tail recursive, nor head recursive**.

Head Recursion

In head recursion, the recursive call is made first, before any processing. All the work happens on the way back up the call stack as the frames unwind.

Example:

```
#include <stdio.h>
void headRecursion(int n) {
```

```
    if (n == 0) return;
headRecursion(n - 1);    // recursive call FIRST
printf("%d ", n);        // processing on the way back
}
int main() {headRecursion(5); return 0; }
// Output: 1 2 3 4 5
```

Since the recursive call comes before **printf**, numbers print in ascending order as the stack unwinds – the opposite of tail recursion.

Example of Fibonacci Series:

```
int fib (int n) {
    if (n == 0)
        return 0;
    else if (n == 1)
        return 1;
    else
        return fib (n - 1) + fib (n - 2);
}
```

Recursion Tree:

```
              Fib (4)
              /   \
         Fib (3)     fib (2)
         /   \      /   \
    Fib (2)  fib (1) fib (1) fib (0)
     /   \
Fib (1)  fib (0)
```

Step	Function Call	Result	Comments
1	fib(4)	fib(3) + fib(2)	expands into two recursive calls
2	fib(3)	fib(2) + fib(1)	left subtree
3	fib(2)	fib(1) + fib(0)	further expands
4	fib(1), fib(0)	1 and 0	base cases
5	fib(2) (right subtree)	fib(1) + fib(0)	again expands
6	fib(1), fib(0)	1 and 0	base cases
	Final Result	fib(4) = 3	(0,1,1,2,3) sequence

Table 7.1: *Step-by-Step Execution of the Recursion Tree*

Quicksort Using Recursion

Quicksort is a highly efficient, comparison-based sorting algorithm that uses a divide-and-conquer approach, and is commonly implemented using recursion. The core idea is to select a 'pivot' element and partition the array around it, then recursively sort the resulting sub-arrays.

```
#include<stdio.h>
// Function to swap two elements
void swap (int *a, int *b) {
    int temp = *a;
    *a = *b;
    *b = temp;
}

// Partition function
    int partition (int arr [], int low, int high) {
     int pivot = arr[high] ;  // choosing last element as pivot
     int i = (low - 1);

    for (int j = low; j < high; j++) {
        if (arr[j] <pivot) {  // if element < pivot
i++;
            swap(&arr[i], &arr[j]);
}
    }
    swap (&arr [i + 1], &arr[high]);
    return (i + 1);
}

// Quick Sort function (recursive)
void quicksort (int arr [], int low, int high) {
    if (low < high) {
        int pi = partition (arr, low, high);

        // Recursively sort elements before and after partition
        quicksort (arr, low, pi - 1);
        quicksort (arr, pi + 1, high);
    }
}

// Function to print array
void printArray (int arr[], int size) {
    for (int i = 0; i < size; i++)
```

```
printf("%d ", arr[i]);
printf ("\n");
}
// Main function
int main () {
    int arr[] = {10, 7, 8, 9, 1, 5};
    int n = sizeof(arr) / sizeof(arr[0]);
printf("Original array: ");
printArray(arr, n);
    quicksort (arr, 0, n - 1);
printf("Sorted array: ");
printArray(arr, n);
    return 0;
}
```

Quick Sort works by selecting a **pivot element** from the array and partitioning the remaining elements into two sub-arrays: one containing elements **less than the pivot,** and the other containing elements **greater than the pivot**. The pivot is then placed in its correct position in the sorted array. This process ensures that the pivot does not need to be considered again.

The same procedure is **recursively applied** to the left and right sub-arrays until each sub-array contains only one or zero elements, which are inherently sorted. To note further, as each partition step reduces the problem size, the algorithm efficiently sorts the entire array.

Complexity Analysis of QuickSort

- **Best Case — O(n log n):** The pivot splits the array into two equal halves at every step, giving a balanced recursion tree of depth log n with O(n) work per level.
- **Average Case — O(n log n):** With a random pivot, partitions are roughly balanced on average, yielding the same O(n log n) growth.
- **Worst Case — $O(n^2)$:** Occurs when the pivot is always the smallest or largest element (for example, already-sorted input). One partition always has n–1 elements, creating a depth-n recursion tree.
- **Space Complexity:** O(log n) on average for the recursive call stack; O(n) in the worst case.

Explanation:

Example Execution

Input Array:

[10, 7, 8, 9, 1, 5]

Step 1: Choose pivot = 5

→ After partition: [1, 5, 8, 9, 10, 7] (Pivot position = 1)

Step 2:

- Left part [1] → already sorted
- Right part [8, 9, 10, 7]

Step 3: Recursive sorting continues until every subarray is sorted.

Final Output:

[1, 5, 7, 8, 9, 10]

Merge Sort Using Recursion

A popular sorting algorithm based on the divide-and-conquer strategy is called merge sort. It operates by repeatedly splitting the supplied array into smaller subarrays until each subarray has a single, naturally sorted element. Following this division procedure, the algorithm compares elements from each half and arranges them in order to merge these subarrays in a sorted fashion. Until every subarray is merged into a single, fully sorted array, this merging procedure is carried out step by step. Large datasets can benefit from Merge Sort's efficiency and guaranteed time complexity of O(n log n).Large datasets can benefit from Merge Sort's efficiency and guaranteed time complexity of O(n log n). However, it is thought to be a drawback because it needs more memory for temporary arrays during the merging process. All things considered, Merge Sort is renowned for its dependability, stability, and consistency.

Merge Sort Example

```
#include <stdio.h>
void merge(int arr[], int left, int mid, int right) {
    int i, j, k;
    int n1 = mid - left + 1;
    int n2 = right   mid;
    int L[n1], R[n2];
    for (i = 0; i < n1; i++)
        L[i] = arr[left + i];
    for (j = 0; j < n2; j++)
        R[j] = arr[mid + 1 + j];
    i = 0; j = 0; k - left;
    while (i < n1 && j < n2) {
        if (L[i] <= R[j]) {
            arr[k] = L[i];
            i++;
        } else {
```

```
            arr[k] = R[j];
            j++;
        }
        k++;
    }
    while (i < n1) {
        arr[k] = L[i];
        i++; k++;
    }
    while (j < n2) {
        arr[k] = R[j];
        j++; k++;
    }
}

void mergeSort(int arr[], int left, int right) {
    if (left < right) {
        int mid = (left + right) / 2;

        mergeSort(arr, left, mid);
        mergeSort(arr, mid + 1, right);

        merge(arr, left, mid, right);
    }
}

int main() {
    int arr[] = {38, 27, 43, 3, 9, 82, 10};
    int n = 7;

    mergeSort(arr, 0, n - 1);

    printf("Sorted array: ");
    for (int i = 0; i < n; i++)
        printf("%d ", arr[i]);

    return 0;
}
```

Power of a Number Using Recursion

To find the power of a number recursively (base^exponent), you define a function that returns the base multiplied by itself (exponent - 1) times, with a base case: if the exponent is 0, return 1 (since any number to the power of 0 is 1). The function calls itself, reducing the exponent by 1 until it hits the base case, then multiplies results back up the call stack.

```
#include <stdio.h>
int power (int base, int exp) {
    if (exp == 0)
        return 1 ;                      // Base case
    else
        return base * power (base, exp - 1) ;  // Recursive case
}
int main () {
    int base, exp;
printf("Enter base: ");
    scanf("%d", &base);
printf("Enter exponent: ");
scanf("%d", &exp);
    int result = power (base, exp);
printf("%d^%d = %d\n", base, exp, result);
    return 0;
}
```

Execution:

```
If we take
Base = 2
Exponent = 4
Power (2, 4)
= 2 * power (2, 3)
= 2 * (2 * power (2, 2))
= 2 * (2 * (2 * power (2, 1)))
= 2 * (2 * (2 * (2 * power (2, 0))))
= 2 * (2 * (2 * (2 * 1)))
= 16
```

Recursion Tree:

```
Power (2, 4)
|
├── power (2, 3)
| ├── power (2, 2)
| | ├── power (2, 1)
| | | └── power (2, 0) = 1
| | └── returns 2
| └── returns 4
└── returns 8
Final result = 16
```

Conclusion

A function that calls itself to solve smaller instances of the same problem is known as recursion, and it is a powerful and elegant programming method. Tree traversals, sorting techniques (like Quick Sort and Merge Sort), and mathematical calculations (like factorial and Fibonacci series) are among the complicated issues it makes simpler. Gaining knowledge of recursion aids in the development of logical reasoning and problem-solving abilities. To prevent excessive memory usage or stack overflow from deep recursive calls, it must be utilized cautiously.

When applied properly, recursion ensures both clarity and efficiency in problem-solving by essentially substituting repeated self-calls for iteration until a base condition is attained.

Exercises

Basic Recursion Exercises

1. Write a recursive function to calculate the factorial of a number.
2. Write a recursive function to print all numbers from 1 to N.
3. Write a recursive function to print all numbers from N to 1.
4. Write a recursive function to calculate the sum of the first N natural numbers.
5. Write a recursive function to check if a number is a palindrome.

Intermediate Recursion Exercises

6. Write a recursive function to calculate the nth Fibonacci number.
7. Write a recursive function to find the Greatest Common Divisor (GCD) of two numbers.
8. Write a recursive function to reverse a string.
9. Write a recursive function to count the number of digits in a number.
10. Write a recursive function to check if an array is sorted.

Advanced Recursion Exercises

11. Write a recursive function to solve the Tower of Hanoi problem.
12. Write a recursive function to find all subsets of a given set (power set).
13. Write a recursive function to calculate the sum of the digits of a number.
14. Write a recursive function to find the minimum element in an array.
15. Write a recursive function to solve a maze (or pathfinding problem).

CHAPTER 8
Structures and Unions

Introduction

In the last chapter, we had discussed Arrays, which can be used in order to store a set of elements. Nonetheless, there is a major drawback in arrays: they are not capable of storing different data types. An example would be that an integer array can hold nothing but integers, whereas, a float array can only contain floating-point numbers. In real life, though, there is hardly ever homogeneous data. The real-life objects tend to be a blend of various types of information. To take an example, assume a Student object of a university database. In order to characterize a student fully, we require:

The student record includes a Name (a string/character array), Roll Number (an integer), Percentage (a float), and Grade (a character).

Assuming we could solve this with arrays, we would have to construct four individual arrays (array of names and roll numbers and so on), and we would have to make sure that index 0 in all arrays are representing the same student. This method renders the program challenging to administer, likely to be erroneous, and challenging to scale.

C offers a remedy to this issue named Structures. A Structure is a pre-defined type of data which enables you to combine together in one name data items of varying types. This enables the modelling of real objects by the programmers. We shall also examine later in this chapter Unions, which are memory-efficient alternatives to structures of particular tasks of the system level.

Structure

In this chapter, we will cover the following topics:

- Defining and Declaring Structures
- Initialization and Accessing Structure Members
- Memory Layout and Structure Padding

- Array of Structures
- Pointers to Structures
- Nested Structures
- Passing Structures to Functions
- Unions and their Memory Management

Defining and Declaring Structures

A **Structure** is a user-defined data type in C that enables the grouping of variables of different data types under a single name. These variables are known as **members** or **fields** of the structure.

Key Characteristics of Structures:

- **Heterogeneous Storage**: Structures are not limited to arrays like other storage types, structures may contain data of various types (int, char, float, arrays, pointers, and the list continues).
- **User-Defined**: The programmer is in charge of defining the data type blue print.
- **Logical Unit**: It considers a set of associated data as one object (such as 'Name, Age, Salary' as one Employee unit).
- **Contiguous Assignment**: Although members appear in a sequential order in the source code, the compiler may insert padding bytes between members to satisfy alignment requirements and improve memory access speed. This padding can increase the overall memory footprint of the structure (this will be discussed in more detail in later sections).

Declaration and Syntax

The development of a structure defines a blue print or a template. It does not assign memory independently. When we declare the variables of that type of structure, it only allocates memory.

Syntax:

```
struct structure_name {
    data_type member1;
    data_type member2;
    ...
data_typememberN;
};
```

- `struct`: The keyword used to define a structure.
- `structure_name`: The tag or name of the structure (such as Student, Car, Book).
- `member`: The variables declared inside the structure.

Example:

```
struct Book {
    char title[50];
    char author[50];
    int pages;
    float price;
};
```

Creating Structure Variables

As soon as the blueprint (structure definition) is prepared, we may make instances (variables) of such a structure. This can be done in two major ways.

Method 1: Declaring with the Definition

Variables may be declared at once after the closing bracket of the structure definition.

```
struct Point {
    int x;
    int y;
} p1, p2;
```

// `p1` and `p2` are variables of type '`struct Point`' created immediately.

Method 2: Declaring inside Main (or Functions)

This is the most common method. You use the struct keyword followed by the tag name to declare variables anywhere in your code.

```
struct Point {
    int x;
    int y;
};

int main() {
    struct Point p1; // Memory allocated for p1
    struct Point p2; // Memory allocated for p2
    return 0;
}
```

Initialization of Structures

Structure variables just like other standard variables can be declared and initialized.

Syntax:

```
struct structure_name variable = {value1, value2, ..., valueN};
```

Example Code:

```
struct Student {
    int id;
    char name[20];
    float marks;
};

// Initialization
struct Student s1 = {101, "John Doe", 88.5};
```

Note: *The order of values in the curly braces {} must match with the order of the members declared in the structure definition.*

Initialization and Accessing Structure Members

After defining and initializing a variable of structure, we require a means through which we can access the separate members of that structure. The name of the structure does not allow us to access the information on the structure as we would like to. We need to specify what particular member in the structure that we are interested in, reading and/or updating.

To accomplish this, C offers Member Access Operator, or often known as the Dot Operator (`.`).

The Dot Operator (.)

The dot operator is used to map the structure variable name and the member name.

Syntax:

```
structure_variable_name.member_name
```

Operations:

- **Reading:** `x = s1.id`; (Reads the value of id from structure s1).
- **Writing:** `s1.id = 200`; (Writes the value 200 into the id member of s1).

Sample Program: Structure Input and Output

This program illustrates the process of declaring a structure, receiving input of the user through the use of a dot operator, and the presentation of the stored data.

```
#include <stdio.h>
#include <string.h>

// Step 1: Define the Structure
struct Employee {
    int id;
    char name[30];
    float salary;
};

int main() {
    // Step 2: Declare the structure variable
    struct Employee emp1;

    // Step 3: Input values using the Dot Operator
printf("Enter Employee ID: ");
scanf("%d", &emp1.id);

    // Consuming the newline character left by scanf
getchar();

printf("Enter Employee Name: ");
    // We can access the array 'name' directly using the dot operator
fgets(emp1.name, sizeof(emp1.name), stdin);

printf("Enter Employee Salary: ");
scanf("%f", &emp1.salary);

    // Step 4: Output values using the Dot Operator
printf("\n--- Employee Details ---\n");
printf("ID: %d\n", emp1.id);
printf("Name: %s\n", emp1.name);
printf("Salary: $%.2f\n", emp1.salary);

    return 0;
}
```

Output:

```
Enter Employee ID: 1001
Enter Employee Name: Alice Smith
Enter Employee Salary: 5500.50
```

```
--- Employee Details ---
ID: 1001
Name: Alice Smith
Salary: $5500.50
```

Program Explanation:

1. **Definition:** We define struct Employee with an integer, a character array, and a float.
2. **Accessing for Input:** **`&emp1.id`** gives the address of the id member variable inside emp1.
3. **String Handling:** **`emp1.name`** refers to the character array. Note that when using **`scanf`** or **`gets`** with a string member, we access it via **`emp1.name`**.
4. **Display:** The **`printf`** statements use **`emp1.id`**, **`emp1.name`**, and **`emp1.salary`** to retrieve the data.

Memory Layout and Structure Padding

The manner in which the structures are stored in memory is one of the most significant notions of C structure programming, and usually baffles a novice programmer.

Contiguous Storage

Structurally, members of the structure are stored in adjacent memories. When one structure variable begins at address 1000, then the members are expected to be placed consecutively after that.

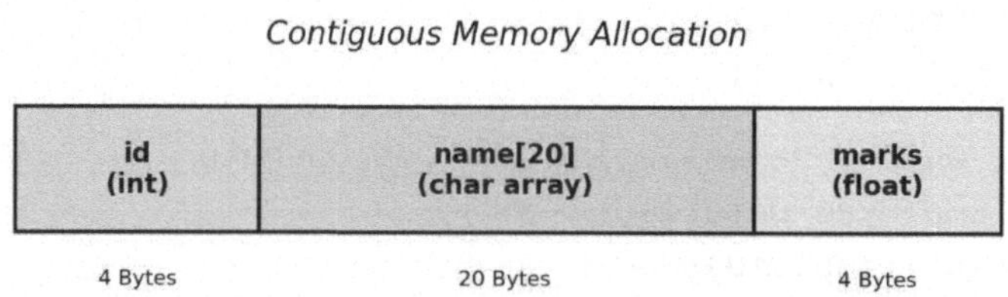

***Figure 8.1**: Structure Memory Layout (Sequential)*

The following figure illustrates the memory layout of a structure in C, showing how member variables are stored at contiguous memory addresses:

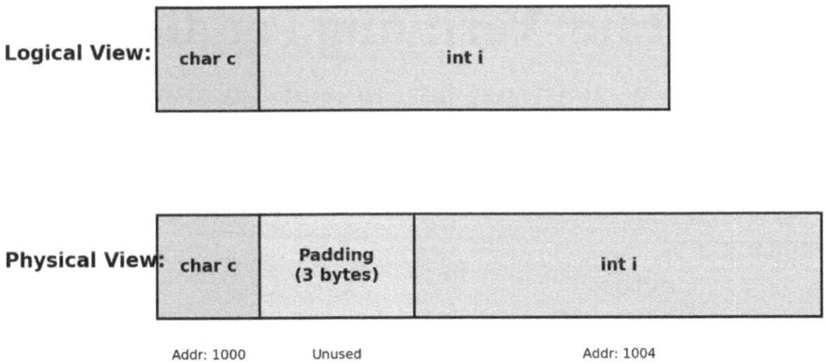

Figure 8.2: *Logical versus Physical Structure*

Structure Padding

As a matter of fact, the size of a structure can be even bigger than the number of the sizes of its members. It is so because of a concept known as Structure Padding, or Alignment.

Memories are read by CPUs in words (usually 4 bytes or 8 bytes at once). The compiler tries to line up the data types to addresses which are multiples of the data type size in order to optimize performance.

- char (1 byte) can start at any address.
- int (4 bytes) usually starts at an address divisible by 4.
- double (8 bytes) usually starts at an address divisible by 8.

If we declare members in an order that violates this alignment, the compiler inserts empty "padding" bytes to force alignment.

Example of Padding:

```
struct Example {
    char c;     // 1 byte
    int i;      // 4 bytes
};
```

Calculation:

1. **c** takes 1 byte.
2. If **i** were stored immediately after **c**, it would start at an odd address (for example, 1001). This is inefficient for the CPU.
3. The compiler inserts **3 padding bytes** after c.
4. i starts at address 1004 (aligned).
5. **Total Size:** 1 (char) + 3 (padding) + 4 (int) = **8 Bytes**.

Sample Program: Verifying Padding

The following program demonstrates how to read and display structure members using standard input functions:

```
#include<stdio.h>

struct NoPadding {
    int i;    // 4 bytes
    char c;   // 1 byte
    // 3 bytes padding likely added at the end for total alignment
};

struct WithPadding {
    char c;       // 1 byte
    double d;     // 8 bytes
    // 7 bytes padding inserted between c and d
};

int main() {
printf("Size of int: %zu\n", sizeof(int));
printf("Size of char: %lu\n", sizeof(char));
printf("Size of double: %lu\n", sizeof(double));

printf("\nSize of struct NoPadding: %lu\n", sizeof(struct NoPadding));
printf("Size of struct WithPadding: %lu\n", sizeof(struct WithPadding));

    return 0;
}
```

Output (on a typical 64-bit compiler):

```
Size of int: 4
Size of char: 1
Size of double: 8

Size of struct NoPadding: 8
Size of struct WithPadding: 16
```

Note: *In **`WithPadding`**, 1 byte is used for char, 7 bytes are wasted (padding), and 8 bytes are used for double. Total = 16 bytes.*

Structure Assignment (Copying)

Structures can be copied unlike arrays which cannot be assigned to each other using the assignment operator =.

Rule:

In case two structure variables are identical in type, it is possible to assign one to another one. In C, struct assignment performs a shallow, member-wise copy. For embedded arrays (such as char name[20]), the array bytes are copied directly into the new struct, which behaves like a deep copy – because the array is a part of the struct itself, and not a pointer to the external memory.

Sample Program: Structure Copy

The following example demonstrates how to declare and use a union in C, illustrating how all members share the same memory location:

```
#include<stdio.h>

struct Point {
    int x;
    int y;
};

int main() {
    struct Point p1 = {10, 20};
    struct Point p2, p3;

    // Method 1: Element-wise copy (Manual)
    p2.x = p1.x;
    p2.y = p1.y;

    // Method 2: Direct Assignment (Automatic)
    p3 = p1;

printf("p1: (%d, %d)\n", p1.x, p1.y);
printf("p2: (%d, %d)\n", p2.x, p2.y);
printf("p3: (%d, %d)\n", p3.x, p3.y);

    return 0;
}
```

Output:

```
p1: (10, 20)
p2: (10, 20)
p3: (10, 20)
```

Explanation:

The statement **p3 = p1**; copies the contents of **p1**'s memory block directly into **p3**. This is significantly easier than copying arrays, where a loop is required.

Array of Structures

We have also seen that one single structure variable can contain data on one object (such as on one student). In practice, however, we seldom have to do with a single object. We frequently must manipulate hundreds or thousands of records, a class roster or library catalog or data base of employees.

As we are able to form an array of integers, so do we form an Arrays of Structures in C.

Definition

An array of structures is a successive sequence of structure variables. The array elements are instances of the entire structures, that is, they hold all the members of the structure blueprint.

Syntax:

```
struct structure_namearray_name[size];
```

Example:

```
struct Student class_X[50];
```

This single line allocates memory for 50 distinct Student structures.

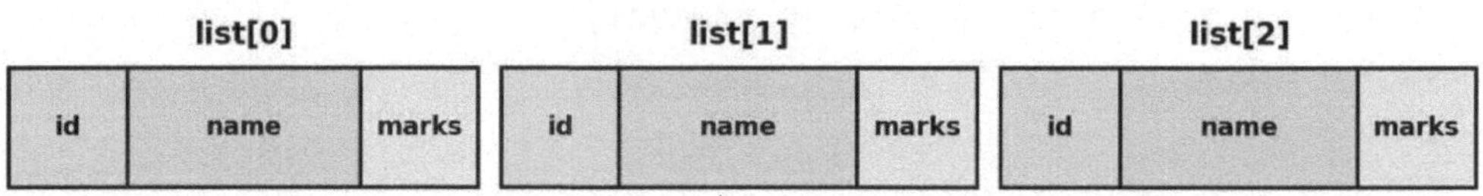

***Figure 8.3:** Memory Layout of struct Student class_X[3]. Notice How the Pattern of Members (ID, Name, Marks) Repeats Sequentially in Memory*

Accessing Array Elements

In order to reference a particular member of a particular structure within the array we add:

1. **Array Subscript [i]**: To select the specific structure instance.
2. **Dot Operator (.)**: To select the specific member inside that instance.

Syntax: `array_name[index].member_name`

Example:

- **`class_X[0].id = 101`**; (Sets the ID of the *first* student).
- **`class_X[4].marks = 92.5`**; (Sets the marks of the *fifth* student).

Sample Program: Creating a Student Database

This program shows the use of an array of structures to form a mini-database. We will record the information of 3 students, and then record the student with the highest marks.

```
#include <stdio.h>

struct Student {
    int roll_no;
    char name[30];
    float marks;
};

int main() {
    // Declare an array of 3 Student structures
    struct Student st[3];
    int i;
    int topper_index = 0;

    // --- Input Phase ---
printf("Enter details for 3 students:\n");
    for(i = 0; i < 3; i++) {
printf("\nStudent %d:\n", i+1);

printf("Enter Roll No: ");
scanf("%d", &st[i].roll_no);

printf("Enter Name: ");
scanf("%s", st[i].name); // No '&' needed for string arrays

printf("Enter Marks: ");
scanf("%f", &st[i].marks);
    }

    // --- Processing Phase (Finding the Topper) ---
    // We assume the first student (index 0) is the topper initially
    for(i = 1; i < 3; i++) {
        if(st[i].marks >st[topper_index].marks) {
topper_index = i; // Update index if we find higher marks
        }
    }

    // --- Output Phase ---
printf("\n--------------------------------\n");
printf("Class Topper Details:\n");
```

```
printf("Name: %s\n", st[topper_index].name);
printf("Roll No: %d\n", st[topper_index].roll_no);
printf("Marks: %.2f\n", st[topper_index].marks);
printf("--------------------------------\n");

    return 0;
}
```

Output:

Enter details for 3 students:

Student 1:

Enter Roll No: 101

Enter Name: Aryan

Enter Marks: 85.5

Student 2:

Enter Roll No: 102

Enter Name: Neha

Enter Marks: 92.0

Student 3:

Enter Roll No: 103

Enter Name: Rahul

Enter Marks: 78.5

Class Topper Details:

Name: Neha

Roll No: 102

Marks: 92.00

Explanation:

1. **Declaration:** struct Student `st[3]` creates three empty slots.
2. **Input:** The loop `for(i=0; i<3; i++)` iterates through indices 0, 1, and 2. We access members using `st[i].member`.
3. **Logic:** We compare `st[i].marks` to find the highest value and store the index of the highest scorer in `topper_index`.

Pointers to Structures

We can have Structures Pointers, just as we can have Characters Pointers and Integers Pointers. This is very vital in fully developed C programming since transferring a large structure to a function by value (copying it) is sluggish. Transfer of a pointer (address) is quick and efficient.

Definition

A **Structure Pointer** is a variable that stores the memory address of a structure variable.

Syntax:

```
struct structure_name *pointer_name;
```

Example:

```
struct Book b1 = {"C Programming", 500};
struct Book *ptr;
ptr = &b1; // 'ptr' now points to 'b1'
The Arrow Operator ()
```

It is an operator, which was introduced to answer structure pointers.

In case we have a variable s1 we will use the dot operator: s1.pages.

When we have a pointer `ptr`, we cannot write `*ptr.pages` because the dot operator has higher precedence than the * operator.

Instead, we have two choices:

1. **Dereference then Dot: `(*ptr).pages`** (Correct but clumsy to type).
2. **Arrow Operator: `ptrpages`** (Preferred, clean syntax).

Rule: `ptrmember` is exactly the same as **`(*ptr).member`**.

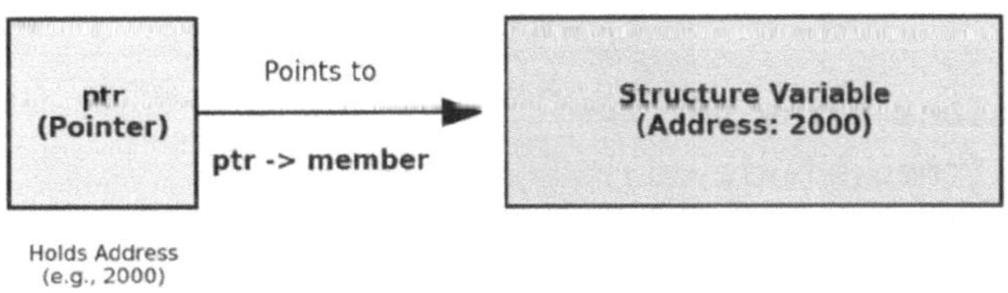

Figure 8.4: *Accessing Structure Members via a Pointer Using the Arrow Operator*

Sample Program: Pointer to Structure

This program illustrates the creation of a structure pointer and alteration of the data in the structure using the structure pointer.

```
#include <stdio.h>

struct Rectangle {
    int length;
    int width;
};

int main() {
    struct Rectangle r1 = {10, 20};

    // Declare a pointer to struct Rectangle
    struct Rectangle *ptr = &r1;

    // Displaying using the pointer and Arrow Operator
printf("Original Dimensions:\n");
printf("Length: %d\n", ptr->length);
printf("Width: %d\n", ptr->width);

    // Modifying the original structure using the pointer
printf("\nUpdating dimensions using pointer...\n");
ptrlength = 50;  // Same as r1.length = 50
ptrwidth = 100;  // Same as r1.width = 100

    // Verify changes in the original variable r1
printf("New Dimensions (checked via r1):\n");
printf("Length: %d\n", r1.length);
printf("Width: %d\n", r1.width);

    return 0;
}
```

Output:

```
Original Dimensions:
Length: 10
Width: 20

Updating dimensions using pointer...
New Dimensions (checked via r1):
Length: 50
Width: 100
```

Why Use Pointers to Structures?

1. **Efficiency:** Structures can be large. If a structure is 1000 bytes, passing it to a function copies 1000 bytes. Passing a pointer copies only 8 bytes (the address).
2. **Dynamic Memory:** When using malloc() to create data structures like Linked Lists or Trees, we *only* deal with pointers to structures.

Nested Structures

A structure may have either members of any type of data, including a structure. When a structure is subordinate to another structure, it is referred to as a Nested Structure. This enables us to have a hierarchical arrangement of data. Consider the definition of an Employee structure. An employee possesses a Name and a Salary. There is also the Date of Joining. A date comprises of a day, month and year. We can separate the day, month and year data within the empathy, and instead of inserting them, we can insert a similar data in a separate date structure and represent this data within the empathy.

Syntax:

```
struct InnerStruct {
    type member1;
    type member2;
};

struct OuterStruct {
    type memberA;
    struct InnerStructnested_variable; // Nesting happens here
};
```

Example:

```
struct Date {
    int day;
    int month;
    int year;
};

struct Employee {
    int id;
    char name[20];
    struct Date doj; // 'doj' is a variable of type struct Date
};
```

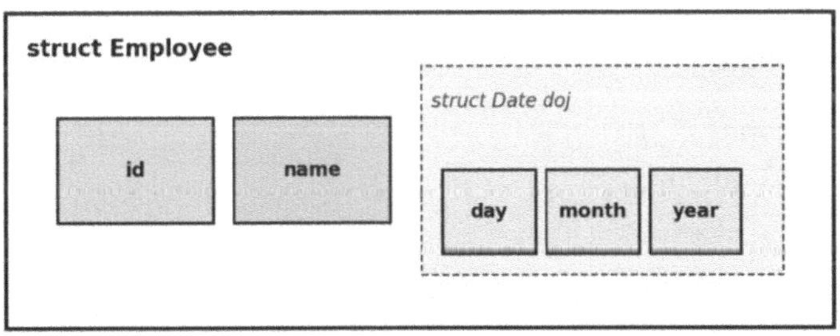

Figure 8.5: *Logical Representation of a Nested Structure. The doj Member inside Employee Expands to Contain Day, Month, and Year*

Accessing Nested Members

To access the inner members, we chain the dot operators.

Syntax: `outer_variable.inner_variable.inner_member`

Example:

- **`e1.id = 101;`** (Accessing outer member)
- **`e1.doj.day = 15;`** (Accessing inner member)
- **`e1.doj.year = 2023;`**

Sample Program: Nested Structures

This program saves and prints the information of an employee that is, his/her address (a nested structure).

```
#include <stdio.h>

// Inner Structure
struct Address {
    char city[20];
    int pin_code;
};

// Outer Structure
struct Person {
    char name[20];
    long long phone;
    struct Address addr; // Nested Structure
};

int main() {
    struct Person p1;

    // --- Input ---
printf("Enter Name: ");
scanf("%s", p1.name);

printf("Enter Phone: ");
scanf("%lld", &p1.phone);

printf("Enter City: ");
scanf("%s", p1.addr.city); // Accessing nested member

printf("Enter Pin Code: ");
scanf("%d", &p1.addr.pin_code); // Accessing nested member
```

```
    // --- Output ---
printf("\n--- Person Details ---\n");
printf("Name: %s\n", p1.name);
printf("Phone: %lld\n", p1.phone);
printf("Address: %s, %d\n", p1.addr.city, p1.addr.pin_code);

    return 0;
}
```

Output:

```
Enter Name: Rohit
Enter Phone: 9876543210
Enter City: Mumbai
Enter Pin Code: 400001
--- Person Details ---
Name: Rohit
Phone: 9876543210
Address: Mumbai, 400001
```

Passing Structures to Functions

Functions enable us to divide the big programs into small manageable functions. In C we can make the same pass of structure variables to functions as we make passes of integers or arrays.

Passing Structures to Functions can be in two ways:

1. **Pass by Value**
2. **Pass by Reference (Using Pointers)**

Pass by Value

In this technique, the whole structure is replicated in the calling function to the called functional.

- **Pros**: Safe. It operates on a duplication, and thus, the original data cannot be accidentally changed.
- **Cons**: Unproductive with big buildings. Replication of a massive system is time, and memory consuming.

Example Code (Pass by Value):

```
void display(struct Student s) { // 's' is a copy
printf("Name: %s\n", s.name);
}
```

Pass by Reference (Using Pointers)

In this approach, there is a passing of the address of the structure only.

- **Pros**: Very efficient. The number of copied bytes is 4 or 8 bytes (the size of a pointer), irrespective of the size of the structure.
- **Cons**: The operation has the power to alter the original data (unless const is used).

Example Code (Pass by Reference):

```
void updateMarks(struct Student *ptr) { // 'ptr' receives an address
ptr->marks = 100; // Modifies original data
}
```

Sample Program: Passing Structures

This program indicates both forms passing by value to print data, and passing by reference to alter data.

```
#include <stdio.h>

struct Item {
    char name[20];
    int price;
};

// Function 1: Pass by Value (Read-only)
void printItem(struct Item i) {
printf("Item: %s, Price: $%d\n", i.name, i.price);
    // Any change to 'i' here would NOT affect the main function
}

// Function 2: Pass by Reference (Modify original)
void applyDiscount(struct Item *ptr) {
    // Reduce price by 10
ptr->price = ptr->price - 10;
}

int main() {
    struct Item myItem = {"Notebook", 50};

printf("Original Details:\n");
printItem(myItem); // Passing entire struct

    // Apply discount
applyDiscount(&myItem); // Passing address

printf("\nAfter Discount:\n");
```

```
printItem(myItem);

    return 0;
}
```

Output:

```
Plaintext
Original Details:
Item: Notebook, Price: $50

After Discount:
Item: Notebook, Price: $40
```

Key Takeaway:

- Pass by Value should be used with small structures or when one only wants to read the data.
- Use Pass by Reference when you have huge structures or when you have to edit the data.

Unions and their Memory Management

In the preceding sections, we have observed the use of structures to enable us to cluster various kinds of data. The only weakness, however with structures is the usage of memory. A structure assigns individual memory to each member.

In very limited memory systems (such as embedded systems or device drivers), we may require a variable that can hold various types of data, but at any given time only one of them. This is a special data type of C known as a Union.

Definition

Union is a user defined data type according to which you can store different types of data in a single memory location.

While a structure can hold an integer **AND** a float **AND** a character simultaneously, a union can hold an integer **OR** a float **OR** a character.

Syntax:

```
union union_name {
    data_type member1;
    data_type member2;
    ...;
};
```

Note: *The syntax is almost identical to a structure, but we use the keyword union.*

Memory Allocation in Unions

This is the key difference.

- **Structure Size:** Sum of the size of all members (plus padding).
- **Union Size:** Equal to the size of the **largest** member.

Example Calculation:

```
union Data {
    int i;          // 4 bytes
    char c;         // 1 byte
    double d;       // 8 bytes
};
```

In the example above, the largest member is double d (8 bytes). Therefore, the total size of union Data is **8 bytes**. All three members (i, c, d) share these same 8 bytes.

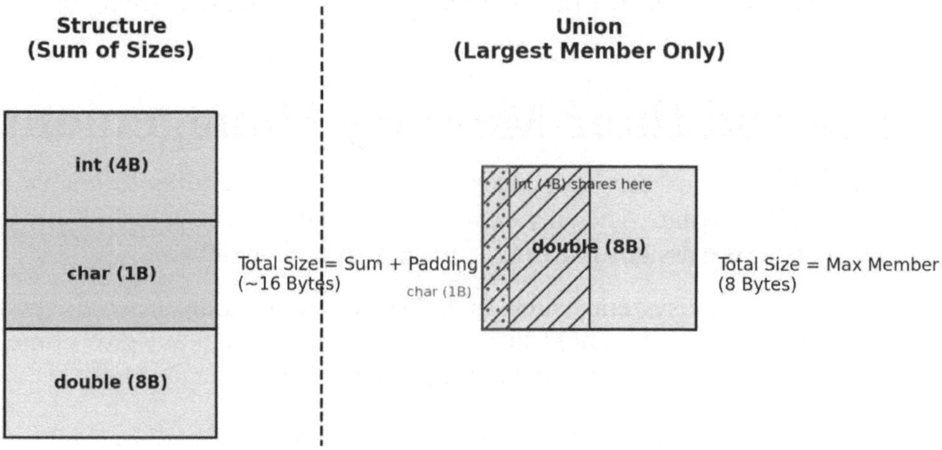

Figure 8.6: *Comparison of Memory Allocation. The Structure Allocates 13 bytes (4+1+8), whereas the Union Allocates only 8 bytes*

Accessing Union Members

Access to union members is done using the same Dot Operator (.). But since they share memory, the others will be overwritten by writing to one of them.

Sample Program: Union Behavior

This program shows the influence of changing one of the members on the rest.

```
#include <stdio.h>
#include <string.h>
```

```
union Data {
    int i;
    float f;
    char str[20];
};

int main() {
    union Data data;

    // Case 1: Assigning and printing one by one (Safe)
data.i = 10;
    printf("data.i: %d\n", data.i);

    data.f = 220.5;
printf("data.f: %.2f\n", data.f);

strcpy(data.str, "C Programming");
printf("data.str: %s\n", data.str);

    // Case 2: The danger of Unions (Corruption)
printf("\n--- Demonstration of Memory Sharing ---\n");

data.i = 10;      // We store an integer
data.f = 220.5;   // We store a float (OVERWRITES the integer)

printf("data.i: %d\n", data.i); // GARBAGE VALUE!
printf("data.f: %.2f\n", data.f); // Correct Value

    return 0;
}
```

Output:

```
data.i: 10
data.f: 220.50
data.str: C Programming

--- Demonstration of Memory Sharing ---
data.i: 1092616192
data.f: 220.50
```

Explanation:

In the case when we put 220.5 into **`data.f`**, it was the binary form of the float that was written into memory. We then attempted to read **`data.ilater`** on, but the computer was now interpreting such float bits as an integer and was giving us a garbage number (1092616192).

Feature	Structure (struct)	Union (union)
Keyword	Struct	Union
Memory Allocation	Allocates memory for **all** members.	Allocates memory for the **largest** member only.
Access	All members can be accessed simultaneously.	Only one member can be accessed at a time.
Value Persistence	Altering one member does not affect others.	Altering one member overwrites the values of others.
Size	Sum of sizes of all members (+ padding).	Size of the largest member.
Usage	Storing distinct attributes (such as Student Record).	Storing mutually exclusive data (for instance, Value is *either* Int *or* Float).

Table 8.1: *Difference between Structure and Union*

Conclusion

One of the important concepts in C programming is the **User-Defined Type** and this is what is used to model intricate real-world objects.

Structures in C are used to group heterogeneous data (variables of different types) under a single name, allowing related information to be managed together as a single unit.

Databases commonly rely on arrays of structures to store and manage collections of records, where each element of the array holds one complete record.

Pointers to structures are essential in dynamic memory allocation and advanced data structures such as linked lists, enabling flexible and efficient memory management.

Unions offer memory-efficient storage by allowing multiple members to share the same memory location, with only one member being accessible at a time.

The next chapter will introduce pointers in C — a powerful feature that enables direct memory access and manipulation, and forms the foundation for dynamic memory allocation and advanced data structures.

Questions

1. Define a Structure in C. How does it differ from an Array?
2. Explain the syntax for declaring a structure with three members: integer, float, and character.
3. What is the Arrow Operator ()? When is it used?

4. Explain the concept of **Structure Padding** with an example. Why does the compiler add padding?
5. Differentiate between Structure and Union with a suitable table.
6. What is a Nested Structure? Write a code snippet to demonstrate it.
7. If a union contains a char (1 byte), an int (4 bytes), and a double (8 bytes), what is the total size of the union?

Programming Exercises

1. **Student Record:** Write a program to create a structure Student with details (Name, Roll No, Marks). Input details for one student and display them.
2. **Library Database:** Write a program to store details of 5 books (Title, Author, Price) using an Array of Structures. Print the details of the most expensive book.
3. **Distance Adder:** Write a program to add two distances (measured in feet and inches) using a structure. (**Hint:** If inches >= 12, increment feet).
4. **Union Size:** Write a program that prints the **`sizeof`** a struct and a union containing the exact same members to demonstrate the difference in memory usage.
5. **Function Update:** Write a function **`updateSalary(struct Employee *e)`** that accepts a pointer to an employee structure and increases the salary by 10%.

CHAPTER 9
Pointers

Introduction

In the previous chapters, we have been taught about the variables that directly store the values. As an illustration, upon typing int a = 10;, the computer allocates a piece of memory and enters 10 in it.

But in the real world, however, we do not usually say much about the value of things, but about their whereabouts. You do not need to know who is in the house at any given time, but rather you just need the address of your friend in case you want to visit him or her. When you obtain the address, you may visit and see what, or who, is inside.

Pointers have been used in C programming to implement this concept. One of the most remarkable and strong characteristics of C is its pointers. They enable applications to connect to memory in the computer. This is what makes C suitable for system-level programming, embedded systems, and operating systems.

Although pointers are potent, they are said to be challenging for novices. In this chapter, the author dissects the concept into uncomplicated, rational steps to make the way C deals with memory less mystical.

Structure

In this chapter, we will cover the following topics:

- Definition and Concepts
- Declaration of Pointers
- Core Operators: & and *
- Sample Program: Basic Pointer Usage
- Why Typed Pointers (int* versus float*)
- Pointer Arithmetic
- Pointers and Arrays

- Functions and Pointers: Call by Reference
- Pointer to Pointer (Double Pointers)
- Generic Pointers (void*)
- NULL Pointers

Definition and Concepts

We have to know the organization of memory to be in a position to know pointers.

Computer memory (RAM) is a large street with millions of houses.

- **Cell:** Every cell is a memory cell (1 byte is usual).
- **Address:** Each house has an address (number) between 0 and the maximum RAM.

On stating that the variable x–50;

- The compiler identifies a free memory address (for example, 1000).
- It records a 50 at that point.

A Pointer is a special variable that is not used to hold a normal value (such as 50 or 3.14). Rather, it stores the memory address of a different variable.

Definition: A Pointer is a variable that contains the address of another variable.

Declaration of Pointers

As in any other variable, a pointer has to be declared. The statement informs the compiler of the type of data that the pointer is going to point to.

Syntax:

```
data_type *pointer_name;
```

Examples:

```
int *p;       // pointer to an integer
float *fp;   // pointer to a float
char *cp;     // pointer to a character
```

Key Note: The asterisk * in the declaration indicates that the variable is a pointer. It is not an operator here; it is a part of the syntax.

Core Operators: & and *

The special operators in the operations of pointers are:

- **The Address-of Operator (&)**

  This is a unary operator that gives back the address of the memory of its operation.

  - If **`var`** is a variable, **`&var`** is the address where **`var`** is stored.
  - Read as: "Address of..."

- **The Dereference Operator (*)**

  It is a unary operator that reads the value of the address that is occupied by the pointer.

  - If **`ptr`** contains the address **`1000`**, then **`*ptr`** retrieves the value stored at address **`1000`**.
  - Read as: "Value at..." or "Value pointed to by..."

The following figure illustrates the relationship between a pointer variable and the memory address it stores, along with the value at that address:

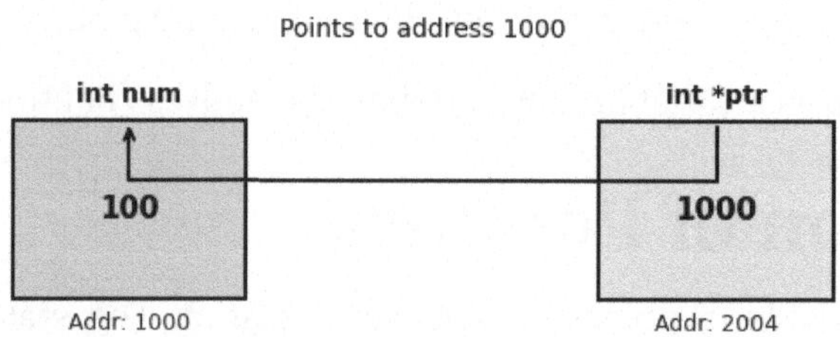

Figure 9.1: *Visualization of a Pointer Variable p Stored at Address 2004, Pointing to Variable x at Address 1000*

Sample Program: Basic Pointer Usage

This program shows the process of declaring a pointer, giving it an address, and the ability to retrieve the value using a pointer.

```
#include<stdio.h>

int main() {
    int num = 100;     // A normal integer variable
    int *ptr;          // A pointer variable that can hold the address of
an int

    // Initialization
ptr = &num;       // Store the address of 'num' in 'ptr'
```

```
    // Printing details
printf("1. Value of num variable: %d\n", num);
printf("2. Address of num (&num): %p\n", (void*)&num);
printf("3. Value stored in ptr:   %p\n", (void*)ptr);
printf("4. Value pointed to by *ptr: %d\n", *ptr);

    // Modifying value via pointer
    *ptr = 200;       // Go to the address in 'ptr' and change value to
200
printf("5. New value of num:      %d\n", num);

    return 0;
}
```

Output (Addresses will vary on different machines):

```
1. Value of num variable: 100
2. Address of num (&num): 0061FF1C
3. Value stored in ptr:   0061FF1C
4. Value pointed to by *ptr: 100
5. New value of num:      200
```

Explanation:

- Line 1 (**ptr = &num**): We put the address of **num** into **ptr**. If num is at address **0061FF1C**, **ptr** now holds the value **0061FF1C**.
- Line 3 (**%p**): The format specifier **%p** is used to print addresses in hexadecimal format. Notice that **&num** and **ptr** print the exact same value.
- Line 4 (***ptr**): This is Dereferencing. The computer looks at **ptr**, sees the address **0061FF1C**, goes to that memory location, and reads the value **100**.
- Line 5 (***ptr = 200**): We used the pointer to remotely change the value of **num**.

Why Typed Pointers (int* versus float*)

You may ask yourself: how come that, with the use of addresses being of the form of a number (hexadecimal value), we have various types of pointers? Why not simply a type of generic pointer?

This is due to Memory Interpretation.

- An **int** typically takes 4 bytes.
- A **char** takes 1 byte.
- A **double** takes 8 bytes.

When you write **`*ptr`**, the compiler needs to know how many bytes to read starting from that address.

- If **`ptr`** is **`int*`**, it reads 4 bytes.
- If **`ptr`** is **`char*`**, it reads 1 byte.

Pointer Arithmetic

Among the most distinctive characteristics of C is the capability to use pointers in arithmetic operations. This is not, however, pointer arithmetic similar to normal integer arithmetic.

In the case of an integer variable val = 1000, val +1 = 1001.

However, when you are pointing to address 1000 with pointer ptr, ptr +1 may give address 1004 or 1008, depending upon the type of data represented.

The Rule of Scaling

When you add or subtract an integer from a pointer, the compiler "scales" the operation by the size of the data type.

Formula:

- For **`char *p`**: `p + 1` increases the address by 1 byte.
- For **`int *p`**: `p + 1` increases the address by 4 bytes (assuming 4-byte integers).
- For **`double *p`**: `p + 1` increases the address by 8 bytes.

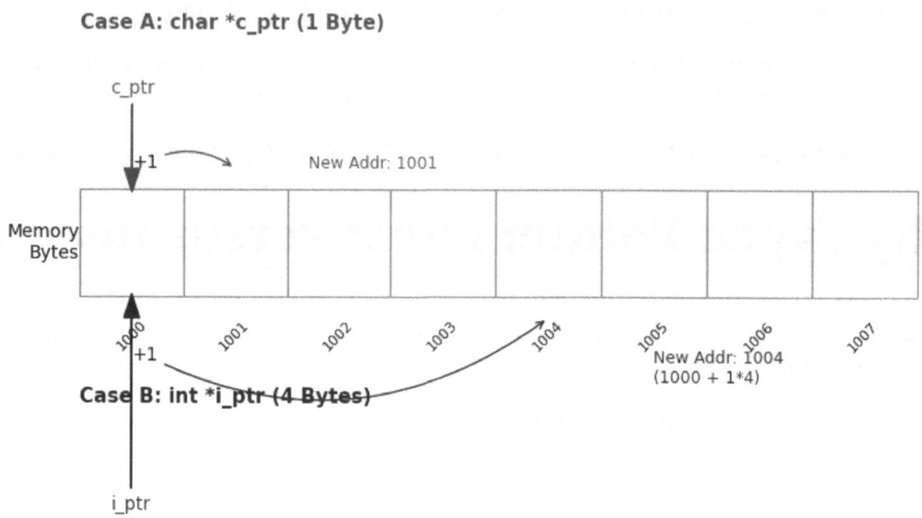

***Figure 9.2:** Visualizing ptr++ for Different Data Types.*
Notice How int Jumps 4 slots, while char* Jumps Only 1*

Valid Operations

The pointers can only be subjected to certain arithmetic operations:

- **Increment/Decrement:** `ptr++`, `ptr--`
- **Addition/Subtraction of Constant:** `ptr + 5`, `ptr - 2`
- **Difference between the Two Pointers ptr2 - ptr1:** Gives the difference between the number of elements between the two pointers.

Invalid Operations:

- Adding two pointers (`ptr1 + ptr2` is illegal).
- Both multiplication and division of pointers.

Sample Program: Pointer Arithmetic

```
#include<stdio.h>

int main() {
    int numbers[] = {10, 20, 30};
    int *ptr = numbers; // Point to the first element (address 1000,
hypothetically)

printf("Original Address: %p\n", (void*)ptr);
printf("Value: %d\n", *ptr);

    // Increment Pointer
ptr++; // Moves to the next integer (Address + 4 bytes)

printf("After ptr++:      %p\n", (void*)ptr);
printf("Value: %d\n", *ptr);

    return 0;
}
```

Output:

Plaintext

```
Original Address: 0061FF10
Value: 10
After ptr++:      0061FF14
Value: 20
```

Notice that the address increased by 4, not 1.

Pointers and Arrays

In C, pointers and arrays can hardly be separated. As a matter of fact, the name of an array is really a constant address of the first element of the array.

The Array Name as a Pointer

If you declare **`int arr[5];`**:

- **`arr`** represents the address of the 0th element.
- **`arr`** is equivalent to **`&arr[0]`**.

Accessing Array Elements

There are two ways of accessing array elements:

- **Array Subscript Notation:** `arr[i]`
- **Pointer Notation:** `*(arr + i)`

The compiler actually converts **`arr[i]`** into **`*(arr + i)`**internally.

Notation	Meaning	Address
`arr[0]`	First element	`arr`
`arr[1]`	Second element	`arr + 1`
`arr[2]`	Third element	`arr + 2`

Table 9.1: *Meaning of Array Presentation*

Sample Program: Traversing an Array Using Pointers

It is a more C-like approach of iterating over an array than the use of an index variable i.

```
#include<stdio.h>

int main() {
    int arr[5] = {10, 20, 30, 40, 50};
    int *ptr;

printf("Traversing array using pointers:\n");

    // Initialize pointer to start of array
ptr = arr;

    for(int i = 0; i < 5; i++) {
printf("Value: %d, Address: %p\n", *ptr, (void*)ptr);
ptr++; // Move pointer to the next element
    }

    return 0;
}
```

Output:

```
Traversing an array using pointers:
Value: 10, Address: 0061FF00
Value: 20, Address: 0061FF04
Value: 30, Address: 0061FF08
Value: 40, Address: 0061FF0C
Value: 50, Address: 0061FF10
```

Functions and Pointers: Call by Reference

Functions used in C can be called in either of the two ways:

1. **Call by Value:** Values of the arguments are cloned to the parameters of the functions.
2. **Call by Reference:** In C, all arguments are passed by value. To allow a function to modify the caller's variable, the variable's address (a pointer) is passed.This is often described as "call by reference" behavior, but technically C is still passing the pointer's value.

The Problem with Call by Value

The default in C is that it uses Call by Value. This implies that when you feed a variable to a function, it manipulates an imitation. Any modifications that are done within the function are lost upon the calling back of the function.

Example (Failed Swap):

```
void swap(int x, int y) {
    int temp = x;
    x = y;
    y = temp;
    // x and y are swapped here, but they are just local copies!
}

int main() {
    int a = 10, b = 20;
    swap(a, b);
printf("a: %d, b: %d", a, b); // Output: a: 10, b: 20 (No Change!)
}
```

The Solution: Call by Reference

In order to adjust the real variables a and b in main, we need to give the addresses of a and b as inputs to the function. This will then be followed by the deregistering of the original memory locations by pointers and the alteration of the original memory locations.

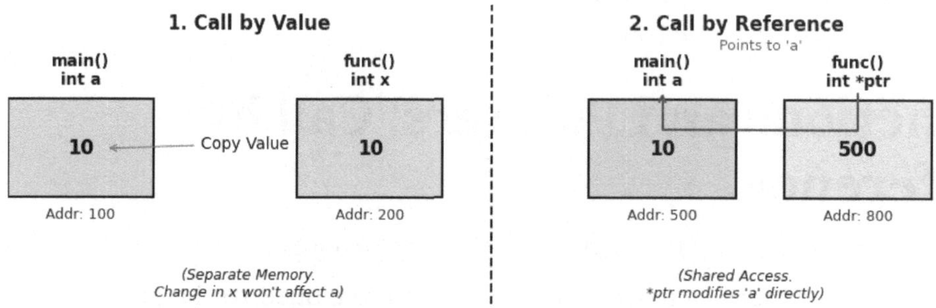

Figure 9.3: *Call by Value Creates Copies (Separate Memory). Call by Reference Passes a Link to the Original Memory*

Corrected Program (Swapping Using Pointers):

```
#include<stdio.h>

// Function accepts pointers (addresses)
void swap(int *x, int *y) {
    int temp;
    temp = *x; // Get value at address x (original a)
    *x = *y;   // Put value at address y into address x
    *y = temp; // Put temp into address y
}

int main() {
    int a = 10, b = 20;

printf("Before Swap: a = %d, b = %d\n", a, b);

    // Pass addresses using & operator
    swap(&a, &b);

printf("After Swap:  a = %d, b = %d\n", a, b);

    return 0;
}
```

Output:

```
Before Swap: a = 10, b = 20
After Swap:  a = 20, b = 10
```

Pointer to Pointer (Double Pointers)

In case a pointer is a variable holding an address, is it possible to have a pointer holding the address of a pointer?

Yes. This is referred to as a Pointer to Pointer (or Double Pointer) Syntax

To declare a pointer to a pointer, we use two asterisks **.

```
int val = 100;
int *ptr = &val;    // Single Pointer
int **pptr = &ptr;  // Double Pointer (points to ptr)
```

Visualization

Imagine a treasure hunt:

1. **Variable (`val`):** The chest of gold (Value: 100).
2. **Pointer (`ptr`):** A map of the location of the chest.
3. **Double Pointer (`pptr`):** This is a map indicating where the initial map is located.

Accessing Values

1. **`pptr`:** Address of **`ptr`**.
2. *pptr: Value of ptr (which is the address of val).
3. **`**pptr`:** Value of **`val`** (100).

Sample Program: Pointer to Pointer

```
#include<stdio.h>

int main() {
    int var = 3000;
    int *ptr;
    int **pptr;

ptr = &var;
pptr = &ptr;

printf("Value of var:   %d\n", var);
printf("Value via ptr:  %d\n", *ptr);
    printf("Value via pptr: %d\n", **pptr);

return 0;
}
```

Generic Pointers (void *)

A special pointer is known as a Void Pointer, which is able to point to data of any type (int, float, char, and struct). It is a "generic" pointer.

Syntax: `void *ptr;`

Limitation: You cannot dereference a void pointer directly because the compiler does not know the size of the data it points to. You must typecast it first.

```
int a = 10;
void *ptr = &a;

// printf("%d", *ptr); // ERROR: Cannot dereference void*
printf("%d", *(int*)ptr); // Correct: Cast to int* then dereference
```

NULL Pointers

A pointer that points at nothing is called a NULL Pointer. As a good practice, always set pointers to null in case you do not allocate one to them. This avoids the Wild Pointers (pointers to arbitrary and dangerous memory addresses).

```
int *ptr = NULL; // Safe initialization
```

Checking for NULL before using a pointer is an essential safety step in C programming:

```
if (ptr != NULL) {
    // Safe to use *ptr
}
```

Dangling Pointers

A dangling pointer is a pointer that once held a valid memory address but no longer does – the memory it points to has been freed, gone out of scope, or otherwise has become invalid. Accessing memory through a dangling pointer produces undefined behavior, which can silently corrupt data or crash the program.

Returning the Address of a Local Variable

Local variables live on the stack and are destroyed when their function returns. A pointer to a local variable becomes dangling as soon as the function exits.

```
int *danglingLocal() {
    int x = 42;          /* local variable on the stack */
    return &x;           /* BAD: x is destroyed after return */
}
/* Fix: return a value, not a pointer to a local */
int safeReturn() { int x = 42; return x; }
```

Pointer to Freed Memory

After calling **free()** on a dynamically allocated block, the pointer still holds the old address. Any subsequent dereference is undefined behaviour.

```
int *p = (int *)malloc(sizeof(int));
*p = 10;
free(p);                  /* memory released */
/* *p = 20;  BAD: p is now dangling */
p = NULL;                 /* Fix: set to NULL immediately after free */
```

Wild (Uninitialized) Pointers

A wild pointer is a pointer that has been declared, but never initialized. It holds a garbage address and dereferencing it is undefined behavior.

```
int *wild;            /* declared but not initialized */
/* *wild = 5;  BAD: wild points to a random address */
/* Fix: always initialize pointers */
int value = 5;
int *safe = &value;  /* points to a known variable */
int *heap = (int *)malloc(sizeof(int)); /* or allocate */
int *none = NULL;    /* or set to NULL if not yet needed */
```

As a rule: every pointer should be NULL, pointing to a valid variable, or pointing to valid heap memory — never uninitialized.

Const Correctness with Pointers

The **const** keyword can be applied in three ways with pointers, and understanding the placement is critical to writing correct, self-documenting C code.

```
const int *p;         /* pointer to const int: value cannot change */
int * const p;        /* const pointer to int: address cannot change */
const int * const p; /* const pointer to const int: neither can change */
```

A useful way to remember the rules: read the declaration from right to left. In const **int *p**, the pointer **p** points-to (*****) a const int — the value is read-only. In **int * const p**, **p** is a **const** pointer to an **int** — the address is fixed but the value can be changed.

```
const int limit = 100;
const int *pLimit = &limit;  /* ok: read-only view */
/* *pLimit = 200;  ERROR: cannot modify a const int through this ptr */
int count = 0;
int * const pCount = &count; /* pCount always points to count */
```

```
*pCount = 5;          /* ok: the value can change */
/* pCount = &limit;  ERROR: cannot change the pointer itself */
```

sizeof Pitfalls: sizeof(ptr) vs sizeof(*ptr)

A very common mistake is using **sizeof** on a pointer when the intention is to get the size of the object it points to. On a 64-bit system, **sizeof(ptr)** is always 8 bytes regardless of what type it points to.

```
int arr[10];
int *p = arr;
/* Wrong way to find array size via pointer */
printf("%zu\n", sizeof(p));     /* prints 8 (pointer size) */
/* Correct: size of the pointed-to type */
printf("%zu\n", sizeof(*p));    /* prints 4 (size of int) */
/* Array size only works on the actual array, not a pointer */
printf("%zu\n", sizeof(arr));  /* prints 40 (10 * 4 bytes) */
```

When an array is passed to a function, it decays to a pointer, so **sizeof** inside the function gives the pointer size, not the array size. Always pass the array length as a separate parameter.

NULL vs 0 in C

In C, **NULL** is a null pointer constant. Depending on which headers are included, it is typically defined as **((void *)0)** or simply 0. Either form is a valid null pointer constant in C, and a pointer initialized to **NULL** is guaranteed never to hold a valid memory address.

```
int *p = NULL;       /* standard: use NULL for pointers */
int *q = 0;          /* also valid in C: 0 is a null pointer constant */
/* NULL and 0 compare equal: */
if (p == NULL) { /* pointer is null */ }
if (!p)        { /* equivalent test */ }
```

Best practice: Always use NULL rather than 0 when working with pointers, as it makes the intent clear to both the compiler, and to other programmers. In C++ (and in C23), the keyword **nullptr** is preferred because it is type-safe – it cannot be accidentally used as an integer.

Conclusion

In summary, pointers are an essential feature of the C programming language that enable efficient memory management and flexible program design. They allow programmers to work directly with memory addresses, making operations on arrays, strings, and dynamic data structures more effective. Pointers play a crucial role in building advanced structures like linked lists, stacks, and queues. While they offer great power and efficiency, they must be used carefully to avoid issues such as memory leaks and invalid access. A clear understanding of pointers is vital for developing optimized and advanced programs. In the next chapter, file handling and string handling topics will be covered.

Questions

1. What is a Pointer? Explain with a memory diagram.
2. Differentiate between the Address-of operator (&) and the Dereference operator (*).
3. What is Pointer Arithmetic? If **`int *p`** is at address 1000, what is the value of `p+1`?
4. Explain the difference between Call by Value and Call by Reference with an example.
5. What is a Double Pointer (**`**ptr`**)? How do you access the final value using it?
6. Why cannot we directly dereference a `void` pointer?

Programming Exercises

1. **Basic Access**: Write a program to print the address of a variable and the value stored at that address using a pointer.
2. **Sum Function**: Write a function **`void sum(int a, int b, int *result)`** that adds `a` and `b` and stores the result in the address pointed to by `result`.
3. **Array Reversal:** Write a program to reverse an array of integers using pointers (no array indices `[]` allowed in the loop).
4. **Max Number**: Write a program using pointers to find the maximum number between two numbers entered by the user.
5. **String Length**: Write a program to calculate the length of a string using a pointer.

CHAPTER 10
File Handling and String Handling in C

Introduction

One significantly limiting factor in all the programs that we have already written, be it calculating grades, sorting arrays, or handling structures, is Data Persistence.

The variables and arrays are saved in the computer's Random Access Memory (RAM) when you run a program. RAM is volatile memory. This is because every bit of that data is killed the moment the program is ended or when the computer is switched off.

Imagine a banking system in which the balances of customers are wiped off whenever the server goes down. That would be catastrophic. In order to create applications in the real world, we must have a permanent method of storing information that can be accessed in the future. This is whereby File Handling comes in.

File Handling enables a program to access data stored in and write information in the secondary storage (Hard Disk, SSD, USB Drive) of the computer. This makes data withstand even the termination of the program.

Structure

In this chapter, we will cover the following topics:

- Definition and Concepts
- Reading and Writing Text Files
- Reading and Writing Binary Files
- Random Access in Files
- Error Handling in File Operations
- String Handling
- Declaration and Initialization of Strings
- Input and Output of Strings

Definition and Concepts

A file is a computer system container for storing information. In C, a file is represented as a stream of bytes pouring in or out of the program.

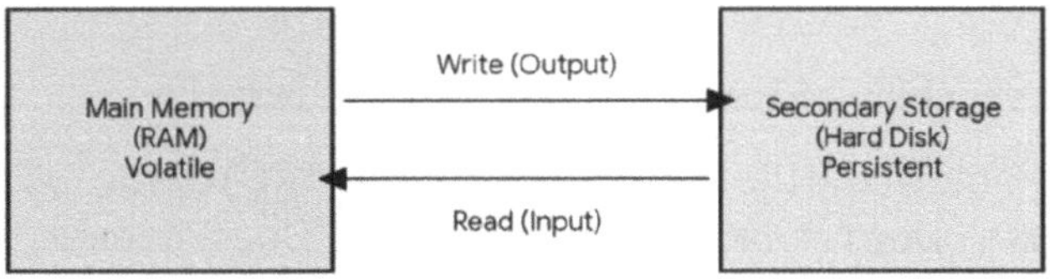

Figure 10.1: *Data Flow between the Main Memory (RAM) and Secondary Storage (Disk)*

Types of Files

Generally, C separates two categories of files:

- **Text Files (`.txt`, `.c`, `.csv`):**
  - Store information in the form of plain characters (ASCII or Unicode).
  - Human-readable. You can open them in TextEdit or Notepad.
  - Newlines are treated in a special way (for example turned into \rn on Windows).
- **Binary Files (`.bin`, `.exe`, `.jpg`, `.dat`):**
  - Record data in the same way it exists in memory (raw 0s and 1s).
  - Not human-readable.
  - More cost-effective in storage and read/write in complex data, such as structures or arrays, faster.

The `FILE` Pointer

In order to handle files within C, we apply a special structure named FILE that is defined in the standard library **<stdio.h>**. This structure contains the information about the file, like the current size, the memory address, and the mode of access.

A variable of type **`FILE`** is not created directly. We instead make use of a pointer to a **`FILE`**.

Syntax:

```
FILE *file_pointer_name;
```

Example:

```
FILE *fp; // 'fp' is a pointer that will hold the reference to a file
```

Opening a File (fopen)

To be able to read or write to a file, we must open it. This makes us have a relationship between our program, and the file on the disk. The function used is **fopen()**.

Syntax:

```
FILE *fopen(const char *filename, const char *mode);
```

- **filename:** Name of the file (for example, "**data.txt**") or the full path (for example, "C:\\Users\\Docs\\data.txt" or "C:/Users/Docs/data.txt").
- **mode:** A string specifying what we want to do with the file (read, write, or append).

The mode parameter is crucial. It tells the Operating System how to treat the file.

Mode	Description	If File Exists	If File Does Not Exist
"r"	**Read**. Open for input operations.	Opens the file.	**Returns NULL** (Error).
"w"	**Write**. Open for output operations.	**Overwrites** (erases) content.	Creates a new file.
"a"	**Append**. Open for adding data at the end.	Preserves content; pointer at end.	Creates a new file.
"r+"	**Read/Write**. Open for both.	Opens the file.	Returns NULL.
"w+"	**Read/Write**. Open for both.	**Overwrites** content.	Creates a new file.
"a+"	**Read/Append**. Open for both.	Preserves content; pointer at end.	Creates a new file.

Table 10.1: *File Opening Modes*

Important Safety Check:

In case of failure (that is, when attempting to read a non-existing file or write to a read-only disk) by **fopen**, one gets a null. It is something you have to always look at.

```
FILE *fp;
fp = fopen("data.txt", "r");

if (fp == NULL) {
printf("Error: Could not open file.\n");
    return 1; // Exit program
}
```

Closing a File (fclose)

You have to close a file once you are done with it. This frees up the memory buffer, and it will be guaranteed that all data is properly written to disk. Opening and forgetting a file may cause corruption of data or leakage of memory.

Syntax:

```
int fclose(FILE *stream);
```

Example:

`fclose(fp);` // Disconnects the file pointer '**fp**' from the file

Sample Program: Creating and Opening a File

This is a simple program that tries to generate a file with the name test.txt. It will print a confirmation message (in case, successful).

```
#include <stdio.h>
#include <stdlib.h> // For exit()

int main() {
    FILE *fp;

    // Attempt to open file in 'w' (Write) mode
    // This will create the file if it doesn't exist
fp = fopen("test_file.txt", "w");

    // Check if the file opened successfully
    if (fp == NULL) {
printf("Error: Failed to create the file.\n");
        exit(1); // Terminate the program with error code
    }

printf("Success: File 'test_file.txt' created/opened successfully.\n");
printf("The file pointer address is: %p\n", (void*)fp);

    // Always close the file when done
fclose(fp);
printf("Success: File closed.\n");

    return 0;
}
```

Explanation:

- **`FILE *fp;`** declares the pointer.
- **`fopen(..., "w")`** asks the OS to create a new file.
- The **`if (fp == NULL)`** block protects the program from crashing if the disk is full or write-protected.
- **`fclose(fp)`** finalizes the operation.

Reading and Writing Text Files

After a file is opened successfully, we can carry out an Input/Output (I/O) operation. C gives three major groups of functions to this, which vary depending on what kind of data we wish to work with:

- **Character I/O: `fputc`** and **`fgetc`**
- **String I/O: `fputs`** and **`fgets`**
- **Formatted I/O: `fprintf`** and **`fscanf`**

Character I/O (`fputc` and `fgetc`)

These are not only the functions of a single character, but also, the most basic types of files I/O.

Writing a Character: `fputc()`

Writes a single character to the stream.

Syntax:

```
int fputc(int char, FILE *stream);
```

- **Returns:** The character written, or End of File (EOF), if there is an error.

Reading a Character: `fgetc()`

Reads the next character from the stream.

Syntax:

```
int fgetc(FILE *stream);
```

- **Returns:** The character read. If the end of the file is reached, it returns a special constant named End of File (EOF).

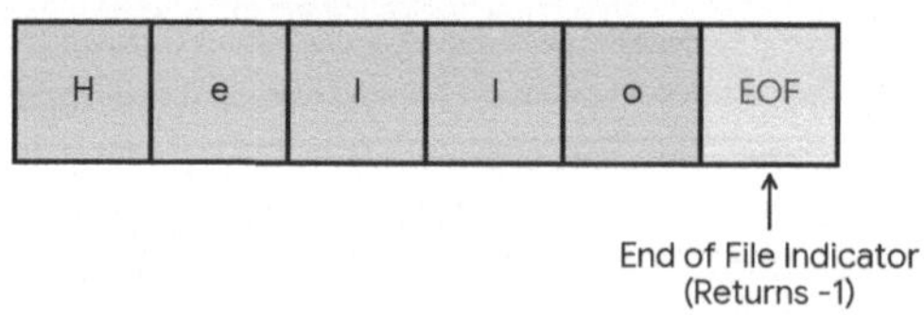

Figure 10.2: *The EOF Marker Indicates the End of Data in a File Stream*

String I/O (`fputs` and `fgets`)

The functions of the strings (lines of text).

Writing a String: `fputs()`

Writes a string to the given file. It does not always introduce a newline at the end.

Syntax:

```
int fputs(const char *str, FILE *stream);
```

Reading a String: `fgets()`

Reads a line of the given file. It ceases with the reading of (n-1) characters, with the reading of the newline character, or the reading of the end-of-file.

Syntax:

```
char *fgets(char *str, int n, FILE *stream);
```

- **str:** Buffer where the string will be stored.
- **n:** Maximum number of characters to read (including the null terminator).
- **stream:** Pointer to the file.

Formatted I/O (`fprintf` and `fscanf`)

These are the **`scanf`** and **`printf`** versions of the file. They enable writing and reading of mixed types of data (integers, floats, strings) without difficulties.

Writing Formatted Data: `fprintf()`

Works exactly like **`printf`**, but the first argument is the file pointer.

Syntax:

```
int fprintf(FILE *stream, const char *format, ...);
```

Reading Formatted Data: `fscanf()`

Works exactly like **`scanf`**, but the first argument is the file pointer.

Syntax:

```
int fscanf(FILE *stream, const char *format, ...);
```

Sample Program 1: Writing to a File

This program demonstrates how to write data using **`fputc`**, **`fputs`**, and **`fprintf`**.

```
#include <stdio.h>
#include <stdlib.h>

int main() {
    FILE *fp;
```

```
    // Open file for WRITING ("w")
    // Warning: This erases existing content in 'output.txt'
fp = fopen("output.txt", "w");

    if (fp == NULL) {
printf("Error opening file.\n");
        exit(1);
    }

// Method 1: fputc (Single Character)
fputc('A', fp);
fputc('\n', fp); // Write a newline

    // Method 2: fputs (String)
fputs("This is a line of text using fputs.\n", fp);

    // Method 3: fprintf (Formatted Data)
    int id = 101;
    float score = 95.5;
fprintf(fp, "Student ID: %d, Score: %.2f\n", id, score);

printf("Data written to 'output.txt' successfully.\n");

fclose(fp);
    return 0;
}
```

File Content (`output.txt`) after Execution:

```
A
This is a line of text using fputs.
Student ID: 101, Score: 95.50
```

Sample Program 2: Reading from a File

The preceding file is read under this program through **`fgetc`**(character by character) up to the End of File (EOF). It is used as the most frequent form of reading complete text files.

```
#include <stdio.h>
#include <stdlib.h>

int main() {
    FILE *fp;
    int ch;  /* fgetc() returns int to correctly represent EOF (-1) */

    // Open file for READING ("r")
fp = fopen("output.txt", "r");
```

```
    if (fp == NULL) {
printf("Error: File 'output.txt' not found.\n");
        exit(1);
    }

printf("--- File Contents ---\n");

    // Loop to read characters until EOF is encountered
    while (1) {
ch = fgetc(fp); // Read one character

        if (ch == EOF) { // Check for End of File
            break; // Exit loop
        }

printf("%c", ch); // Print character to console
    }

printf("\n--- End of File ---\n");

fclose(fp);
    return 0;
}
```

Explanation:

- **`fp = fopen(..., "r")`**: Opens the file in read mode.
- **`while(1)`**: An infinite loop that continues reading.
- **`ch = fgetc(fp)`**: Fetches the next byte from the file.
- **`if (ch == EOF)`**: The critical check. EOF is a constant (usually -1) defined in <stdio.h> that signals no more data is available.
- **`printf("%c", ch)`**: Displays the character on the screen.

Console I/O Function	File I/O Function	Destination/Source
`printf("Hello");`	`fprintf(fp, "Hello");`	Writes to Screen versus Writes to File
`scanf("%d", &vars);`	`fscanf(fp, "%d", &vars);`	Reads from Keyboard versus Reads from File

Table 10.2: *Comparison: `printf/scanf` versus `fprintf/fscanf`*

Reading and Writing Binary Files

Until now, we have been subject to the Text Files, that is, data that is represented in readable forms. Text files, although easy to read, are however, limited:

- **Inefficiency:** A text file (1 byte per character: '1', '2'...) can hold the integer 123456 using 6 bytes, whereas using only 4 bytes in memory (as a raw integer) is possible.
- **Precision Loss:** Floating- point numbers can lose precision as they are represented as text.

Binary Files address this by providing data in the computer as it appears in the computer memory (RAM). Two potent functions are required to operate an input/output in binary mode: **`fwrite()`** and **`fread()`**.

Writing Binary Data: `fwrite()`

This function creates a block of memory in the file.

Syntax:

```
size_tfwrite(const void *ptr, size_t size, size_t count, FILE *stream);
```

- `ptr`: Pointer to the block of memory to be written (like an address of a structure).
- `size`: Size of each element (such as **`sizeof(struct Student)`**).
- `count`: Number of elements to write (for instance, 1 for a single variable, 50 for an array).
- `stream`: The file pointer.

Reading Binary Data: `fread()`

This operation recovers a block of memory from the file into a variable.

Syntax:

```
size_tfread(void *ptr, size_t size, size_t count, FILE *stream);
```

- **Returns:** The number of elements successfully read. If this is less than count, it indicates either an error, or the End of File (EOF).

Sample Program: Writing Structures to a Binary File

This is the most widespread binary file application: one can save a complete database of structures simultaneously.

Note: *We must open the file in* **binary mode** *("**wb**" for write binary, "**rb**" for read binary).*

```
#include<stdio.h>
#include <stdlib.h>
```

```
struct Student {
    int id;
    char name[20];
    float marks;
};

int main() {
    FILE *fp;
    struct Student s1 = {101, "Alice", 92.5};
    struct Student s2 = {102, "Bob", 88.0};

    // Open file in "wb" (Write Binary) mode
fp = fopen("students.dat", "wb");

    if (fp == NULL) {
printf("Error creating file.\n");
        exit(1);
    }

    // Write the structures directly to the file
      // Arguments: (address of data, size of one element, number of elements, file pointer)
fwrite(&s1, sizeof(struct Student), 1, fp);
fwrite(&s2, sizeof(struct Student), 1, fp);

printf("Data written to 'students.dat' successfully.\n");

fclose(fp);
    return 0;
}
```

What is students.dat?

When you attempt to open students.dat in Notepad, it will appear as a meaningless mass of garbage or gibberish, since it is not a text file, but binary data.

Sample Program: Reading Structures from a BinaryFile

In order to interpret the binary data, we have to reinterpret it back into the same format of structure using a C program.

```
#include <stdio.h>
#include <stdlib.h>

struct Student {
    int id;
```

```
    char name[20];
    float marks;
};

int main() {
    FILE *fp;
    struct Student temp;

    // Open file in "rb" (Read Binary) mode
fp = fopen("students.dat", "rb");

    if (fp == NULL) {
printf("Error: File not found.\n");
        exit(1);
    }

printf("--- Reading from Binary File ---\n");

    // Loop until fread returns 0 (End of File)
    while(fread(&temp, sizeof(struct Student), 1, fp) == 1) {
printf("ID: %d, Name: %s, Marks: %.2f\n", temp.id, temp.name, temp.
marks);
    }

fclose(fp);
    return 0;
}
```

Output:

```
--- Reading from Binary File ---
ID: 101, Name: Alice, Marks: 92.50
ID: 102, Name: Bob, Marks: 88.00
```

Feature	Text Mode ("r", "w")	Binary Mode ("rb", "wb")
Newlines	Converts \n to \r\n (on Windows).	No conversion. Exact byte copy.
Data Storage	Stores data as characters (ASCII).	Stores raw memory bits (0s and 1s).
Readability	Human-readable.	Not human-readable.
Efficiency	Slower (requires conversion).	Faster (direct memory copy).
Usage	.txt, source code, logs.	Images, audio, and structure databases.

Table 10.3: *Text Mode versus Binary Mode*

In C programming, file handling enables data to be permanently stored in files. When working with files, data can be handled in two different modes: text mode and binary mode. These modes control how data is saved, accessed, and interpreted by the system.

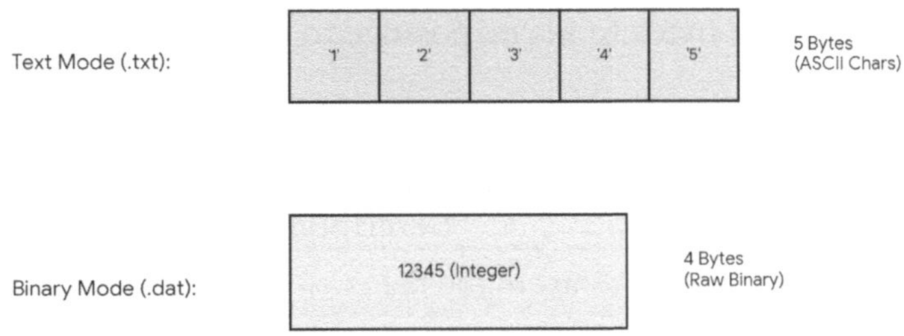

Figure 10.3: *Comparison of How the Number 12345 is Stored in Text Mode (5 bytes: ASCII Characters) versus Binary Mode (4 bytes: Integer Value)*

Random Access in Files

So far, we have performed **Sequential Access**. This implies that to read the 100th byte in a file, we had to read the 99 files that came before it. Well, it is as much like a cassette tape, as you have to reel through all the stuff to get to the song you need.

Random Access enables us to skip to any byte of the file like a CD or hard drive track. C offers these three principally in terms of:

- `rewind()`
- `ftell()`
- `fseek()`

`rewind()`

Sets the file pointer back to the beginning of the file.

Syntax:

```
void rewind(FILE *stream);
```

`ftell()`

Returns the current position of the file pointer (in bytes from the beginning). This comes in handy when searching for your position in a file or determining the overall size of a file.

Syntax:

```
long ftell(FILE *stream);
```

`fseek()`

Moves the file pointer to a specific location.

Syntax:

```
int fseek(FILE *stream, long offset, int origin);
```

- **offset**: Number of bytes to move (positive to move forward, negative to move backward).
- **origin**: The starting point for the move.

Constant	Description
SEEK_SET	Start of the file.
SEEK_CUR	Current position of the pointer.
SEEK_END	End of the file.

Table 10.4: *C Defines Three Constants for This*

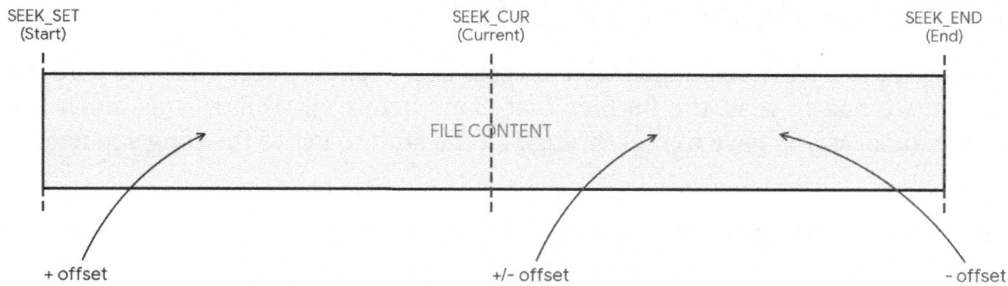

Figure 10.4: *Visualizing fseek Movements — SEEK_SET + 10 Jumps to Byte 10. SEEK_END - 5 Jumps to 5 Bytes before the End*

Sample Program: Random Access

In this program, a string is written in a file, followed by the **fseek** used to move backwards and overwrite a section of the file.

```
#include<stdio.h>
#include<stdlib.h>

int main() {
    FILE *fp;

fp = fopen("random.txt", "w+"); // w+ allows both reading and writing
    if (fp == NULL) exit(1);

    // 1. Write initial text
fputs("This is a simple file.", fp);

    // Current Content: "This is a simple file."
    // Pointer is at the end.

    // 2. Move pointer 5 bytes backward from the current position
fseek(fp, -5, SEEK_CUR);
```

```
    // 3. Overwrite "file." with "text."
fputs("text.", fp);

    // 4. Move to the beginning to print the whole file
    rewind(fp);

printf("Updated Content: ");
    char ch;
    while((ch = fgetc(fp)) != EOF) {
printf("%c", ch);
    }

    // 5. Find file size using fseek/ftell trick
fseek(fp, 0, SEEK_END); // Jump to end
    long size = ftell(fp);  // Get position (which equals file size)
printf("\nTotal Size: %ld bytes\n", size);

fclose(fp);
    return 0;
}
```

Output:

```
Updated Content: This is a simple text.
Total Size: 22 bytes
```

Error Handling in File Operations

There is a high probability of file operations errors (some of which includes disk full, file missing, and permission denied). The standard mechanisms to detect these errors are supplied by C.

`feof()`

Checks if the End-of-File indicator has been set.

```
if (feof(fp)) {
printf("End of file reached.\n");
}
ferror()
```

Checks if an error indicator has been set for the file (such as hardware read error).

```
if (ferror(fp)) {
printf("Error reading from file.\n");
}
```

String Handling

In C programming language, a string is defined as a sequence of characters stored in a character array, and it is always terminated by a special character known as the null character ('\0'). This null character marks the end of the string, and allows C to determine where the string finishes in memory. Without '\0', C cannot identify the end of a string, which may lead to unexpected behavior or memory errors.

Unlike many high-level languages such as Python, Java, or C++, C does not provide a built-in string data type. Instead, strings are handled using arrays of type char. Each element of the array stores a single character, and the final element must be the null character. For example, the string "Hello" is stored in memory as:

'H' 'e' 'l' 'l' 'o' '\0'

Since C lacks native string support, it relies on standard library functions for performing common string operations. These functions are declared in the header file **`<string.h>`**. The library provides functions to perform tasks such as finding the length of a string (**`strlen()`**), copying strings (**`strcpy()`**), concatenating strings (**`strcat()`**), and comparing strings (**`strcmp()`**).

String handling in C, therefore requires careful attention to memory management. The programmer must ensure that the character array has sufficient size to store the string along with the terminating null character. Improper handling—such as missing the null terminator or exceeding array bounds—can result in buffer overflows and undefined behavior.

In summary, string handling in C is based on character arrays and library functions, making it powerful and flexible, but also more error-prone compared to languages with built-in string types. Proper use of **`<string.h>`** functions and safe programming practices is essential for reliable string manipulation in C.

Declaration and Initialization of Strings

```
 char str1[20];                    // Declaration
char str2[20] = "Hello";          // Initialization
char str3[] = { 'H', 'e', 'l', 'l', 'o', '\0' };
char str4[] = "Welcome to C";
```

Input and Output of Strings

In C, strings are handled as character arrays, and a special care is required while taking input and displaying output. Different functions are available for string input and output, each with its own use case and limitations.

`scanf()` Function

Purpose:

`scanf()` is used to take formatted input from the keyboard.

Syntax:

```
scanf("format_specifier", variable);
```

Using scanf() with Strings:

```
char str[20];
scanf("%s", str);
```

How it Works

- Reads characters until it encounters a **whitespace** (space, tab, or newline).
- Automatically appends the null character '`\0`' at the end.

Advantages:

- Simple and fast.
- Useful for single-word input.

Limitations

- Cannot read strings with spaces.
- No built-in size checking → risk of buffer overflow.

Example

```
char name[20];
printf("Enter name: ");
scanf("%s", name);
printf("Name: %s", name);
```

`gets()` Function (Unsafe / Deprecated)

Purpose

`fgets()` reads a line of text from standard input.

Syntax

```
gets(str);
```

How it Works

- Reads input until a newline is encountered.
- Removes the newline and appends '\0'.

Advantages

- Can read strings containing spaces.

Limitations

- Extremely unsafe.
- It does not check the array size.
- Can cause buffer overflow.
- Removed from C11 standard.

Example

```
char sentence[50];
fgets(sentence, sizeof(sentence), stdin);
puts(sentence);
```

To make a note, use of **`gets()`** is strongly discouraged.

`puts()` Function

Purpose:

`puts()` is used to **output a string** to the screen.

Syntax:

```
puts(str);
```

How it Works:

- Prints the string until '**`\0`**' is found.
- Automatically adds a **newline** at the end.

Advantages:

- Simple and easy to use.
- Automatically moves to the next line.

Limitations:

- Cannot format output (unlike **`printf()`**).

Example

```
char msg[] = "Welcome to C programming";
puts(msg);
```

Common String Handling

In C, string handling is performed using the standard library functions declared in the header file **`<string.h>`**. These functions help in performing operations such as finding length, copying, concatenation, comparison, and searching within strings.

Function	Purpose
strlen(str)	Returns length of string.
strcpy(dest, src)	Copies one string to another.
strncpy(dest, src, n)	Copies first n characters.
strcat(dest, src)	Concatenates two strings.
strcmp(str1, str2)	Compares two strings.
strncmp(str1, str2, n)	Compares first n characters.
strchr(str, ch)	Finds first occurrence of a character.
strstr(str, sub)	Finds substring.

Table 10.5: *Table Showing String Function and its Purpose*

C Program Using Common String Functions

```
#include <stdio.h>
#include <string.h>

int main() {
    char str1[50] = "C Programming";
    char str2[50] = " Language";
    char str3[50];
    char str4[50] = "C Programming";
    char *ptr;

    /* 1. strlen() */
printf("Length of str1: %lu\n", strlen(str1));

    /* 2. strcpy() */
strcpy(str3, str1);
printf("After strcpy, str3: %s\n", str3);

    /* 3. strcat() */
strcat(str1, str2);
printf("After strcat, str1: %s\n", str1);

    /* 4. strcmp() */
    if (strcmp(str3, str4) == 0)
printf("str3 and str4 are equal\n");
    else
printf("str3 and str4 are not equal\n");

    /* 5. strncpy() */
strncpy(str3, str2, 4);
```

```
    str3[4] = '\0';   // ensure null termination
printf("After strncpy, str3: %s\n", str3);

    /* 6. strncat() */
strncat(str3, str4, 5);
printf("After strncat, str3: %s\n", str3);

    /* 7. strchr() */
ptr = strchr(str4, 'P');
    if (ptr != NULL)
printf("Character 'P' found at position: %ld\n", ptr - str4);

    /* 8. strrchr() */
ptr = strrchr(str4, 'g');
    if (ptr != NULL)
printf("Last occurrence of 'g' at position: %ld\n", ptr - str4);

    /* 9. strstr() */
ptr = strstr(str4, "Program");
    if (ptr != NULL)
printf("Substring \"Program\" found\n");

    return 0;
}
```

C Program without Using Common String Functions

```
#include <stdio.h>
int main() {
    char str1[50] = "C Programming";
    char str2[50] = " Language";
    char copy[50];
    char concat[100];
    int i, j, len1 = 0, len2 = 0;

    /* 1. Find length of str1 */
    while (str1[len1] != '\0') {
        len1++;
    }
printf("Length of str1 = %d\n", len1);

    /* 2. Copy string */
    i = 0;
    while (str1[i] != '\0') {
        copy[i] = str1[i];
i++;
```

```
    }
    copy[i] = '\0';
printf("Copied string = %s\n", copy);

/* 3. Concatenate strings */
    i = 0;
    while (str1[i] != '\0') {
        concat[i] = str1[i];
        i++;
    }

    j = 0;
while (str2[j] != '\0') {
concat[i] = str2[j];
        i++;
        j++;
    }
    concat[i] = '\0';
printf("Concatenated string = %s\n", concat);

/* 4. Compare strings */
    i = 0;
    while (str1[i] != '\0' && str2[i] != '\0' && str1[i] == str2[i]) {
i++;
    }

    if (str1[i] == str2[i])
printf("Strings are equal\n");
    else
printf("Strings are not equal\n");

    /* 5. Reverse string */
    i = 0;
    while (str1[i] != '\0') {
        i++;
    }
    i--;   // move to last character

printf("Reversed string = ");
    while (i >= 0) {
printf("%c", str1[i]);
        i--;
}
    return 0;
}
```

Conclusion

File manipulation converts C programs of temporary calculators into long-term systems that are able to manage data. Text Files are excellent when it comes to human readability and easy logs. Binary Files are necessary when efficiency and storage of complex structures are needed. Random Access functions (`fseek`, `ftell`) enable the manipulation of data, which is important in the development of applications such as a database engine or media player.

File handling and string handling are deeply interconnected in C. Files store data as sequences of bytes, and when that data represents text, programs must read it into character arrays — that is, C strings — before processing it. The same `<string.h>` functions used to manipulate in-memory strings are therefore indispensable when working with file content: parsing lines read with `fgets()`, formatting output written with `fprintf()`, or searching through filenames and paths. The following section covers the string handling facilities that complement the file I/O techniques explored above.

In C programming, string handling without using built-in string functions highlights the **fundamental concept that strings are simply character arrays terminated by the null character** ('\0'). By manipulating strings manually using loops and conditional statements, we gain a clear understanding of how common string operations—such as finding length, copying, concatenation, comparison, and reversal—work internally.

Questions

1. Why is file handling necessary in programming?
2. Differentiate between Text Mode and Binary Mode file operations.
3. What is a File Pointer? Which structure does it point to?
4. Explain the purpose of the `fopen()` function. List three common file opening modes.
5. What does EOF stand for?
6. Explain the usage of `fseek()` with its three arguments.
7. Write a C program to find the length of a string.
8. Write a C program to copy one string to another string.
9. Write a C program to concatenate two strings.
10. Write a C program to compare two strings.
11. Write a C program to convert lowercase string to uppercase.
12. Write a C program to convert uppercase string to lowercase.

13. Write a C program to toggle case of each character of a string.
14. Write a C program to find total number of alphabets, digits or special character in a string.
15. Write a C program to count total number of vowels and consonants in a string.
16. Write a C program to count total number of words in a string.
17. Write a C program to find reverse of a string.
18. Write a C program to check whether a string is palindrome or not.
19. Write a C program to reverse order of words in a given string.

Programming Exercises

1. **File Copy:** Write a program to copy the contents of one file (source.txt) to another (`destination.txt`).
2. **Count Characters:** Write a program to count the number of characters, spaces, and newlines in a file.
3. **Merge Files:** Write a program that reads two text files and merges them into a third file.
4. **Student Database (Binary):** Create a program that writes an array of 5 Student structures to a binary file, then reads the 3rd student record directly using `fseek` and prints it.
5. **Reverse File:** Write a program to read a text file and print its content in reverse order (last character first) using `fseek` and `ftell`.

Index

A

actual parameters 75, 76
Address-of Operator (&) 124
algorithm
  about 11
  aspect 13
  characteristics 12, 60
  classification 62
  data type 14
  example 12
  examples 62
  flowchart 13
  representations 61
  variable 13
algorithm, example
  searching algorithm 62
  sorting algorithm 65
alignment 105
argument list 75
arithmetic operators
  about 23, 24
  bitwise operator 27, 28
  logical operator 25-27
  relational operator 25-27
  relational operators, working 24
arithmetic pointer
  about 126
  scaling rule 126
  valid operations 127
array
  about 47, 127
  applications 47
  characteristics 47
  defining 47
  element, accessing 47, 48
  elements, accessing 128
  traversing, with pointer 128
array elements
  accessing 108
array of structures
  about 108
  array elements, accessing 108
  defining 108
  student database, creating 109, 110
array pointers
  about 56-58
  applications 57
  program 56
array traversal
  about 53
  applications 54
  duplicate number, findings with 1D array 55
  program 54
  with recursion 55
  with two pointers 54
Assembler 11
Asymptotic Notation
  about 67

Big-O Notation (O) 68
Omega Notation (Ω) 68, 69
Theta Notation (Θ) 69
types 68
automatic variables 82

B

base case 88
Basic Combined Programming Language (BCPL) 1
batch operating system 8
Big-O Notation (O) 68
binary files
about 137
binary data, reading 144
binary data, writing 144
reading 143, 144
structures, reading 145, 146
structures, writing 144, 145
writing 143, 144
Binary Search 63, 65
bitwise operator 27, 28
branching
about 33
components 38
conditional (ternary) operator 35, 36
do-while loop 39
do-while loop program 43
if statement 33
infinite loop 41
leap year 42
nested if-else statement 34, 35
palindrome 42, 44
post-increment operator (i++) 41
pre-increment operator (++i) 41
switch statement 36, 37
while loop 38
bubble sort 65, 66

C

call by address
about 79, 80
variable life span 81
variable scope 80
call by value 78-80
called function 76-78
calling function 76-78
character I/O
fgetc() 140
fputc() 140
Compiler
about 11
function 11
complexity
about 66
example 67
space complexity 66
time complexity 66
use cases 67
computer system
advantages 7
common uses 7
components 3
data 6
disadvantages 7
key features 7
main components 5, 6
networking components 6
peopleware 6
software 6
computer system, components
arithmetic and logic unit (ALU) 3, 4
central processing unit (CPU) 3
computer velocity attributes 5
control unit 4
input unit 3
memory registers 4
motherboard 4
output unit 4
power supply unit (PSU) 5
random access memory (RAM) 5
conditional (ternary) operator 35, 36
constants
about 20
printf conversion specifier 22
symbolic constants 21, 22

const keyword 133
contiguous storage 104
C program
  without string functions 154
  with string functions 153
C programming language
  about 1, 2
  features 2, 3

D

dangling pointer
  about 132
  free memory 133
  local variable address, returning 132
data type
  about 14
  example 15
  format 14
  in C 14
  output window 15
declarations 22, 23
Dereference Operator (*) 124
direct recursion 89, 90
Distributed Operating System (DOS) 9
dot operator (.) 102
Double Pointer
  about 131
  values, accessing 131
  visualization 131
do-while loop
  about 39
  features 40
  key points 40
  working 40
dummy parameters 75
dynamic programming
  about 69, 70
  technique 70

E

Embedded Operating System 10
error handling
  in file operations 149
exponent
  about 96
  recursion tree 97
  recursion, using 96

F

fgetc() 140
fields 100
file
  creating 139
  opening 139
file closing (fclose) 138
file opening (fopen) 138
file operations
  error handling 149
file pointer 137
file random access
  about 147
  fseek() 147, 148
  ftell() 147
  program 148
  rewind() 147
files types
  binary files 137
  text files 137
file types 137
formal parameters 75, 76
formatted I/O 141
fputc() 140
fread() 144
function call 75
function declaration
  about 75
  syntax 75
function definition
  about 74
  function body 74
  function header 74
functions
  about 129
  call by reference 130
  call by value 129
  categories 76

functions types
  about 73, 89
  direct recursion 89, 90
  head recursion 91, 92
  indirect recursion 90
  library functions 74
  no tail/head recursion 91
  tail recursion 91
  user-defined functions (UDFs) 74
fwrite() 144

G

gets() function
  about 151
  advantages 152
  limitations 152
  syntax 151
  working 151
global scope 80, 81
global variables 81

H

Hard Disk Drive (HDD) 6
head recursion
  about 91, 92
  Fibonacci series, example 92
  recursion tree 92

I

identifiers 18, 21
if statement 33
indirect recursion 90
infinite loop 41
Interpreter 11
invalid operations 127

L

leap year 42
library functions 74
Linear Search 63
local scope 81
local variables 82
logical operator 25, 27

M

matrix chain multiplication 70, 71
members 100
merge sort
  about 95
  recursion, using 95
Mobile Operating System 9
Multi-Dimensional (MD) array 52, 53
Multiprocessing Operating System (MPU OS) 10
Multitasking Operating System 8
Multi-User Operating System 10

N

nested if-else statement 34, 35
Nested Structure
  about 113
  accessing 114
  program 114
Network Operating System (NOS) 9
no tail/head recursion 91
null pointer
  about 132
  versus void (0) 134

O

Omega Notation (Ω) 68, 69
one-dimensional (1D) array 48, 49
operating system 7, 8
operators
  about 124
  Address-of Operator (&) 124
  Dereference Operator (*) 124

P

parameters passing
  call by address 79
  call by value 78, 79
  to functions 78
pass by reference
  about 116
  cons 116

pros 116
pass by value
about 115
cons 115
pros 115
passing structures to functions
about 115
pass by reference 116
pass by value 115
program 116, 117
pointer
about 123, 127
array name 128
declaring 123
usage 124, 125
post-increment operator (i++) 41
pre-increment operator (++i) 41
printf conversion specifier 22
puts() function
about 152
advantages 152
limitations 152
string handling 152
syntax 152
working 152

Q

Quicksort
about 93
complexity analysis 94, 95
recursion, using 93, 94

R

Real-Time Operating System (RTOS) 9
recursion
using, in exponent 96
using, in merge sort 95
using, in Quicksort 93, 94
register variables 83
relational operators
about 25
working 24

S

scanf() function
about 151
advantages 151
limitations 151
syntax 151
using, with strings 151
working 151
searching algorithm
Binary Search 63, 65
Linear Search 63
searching algorithms 62
Single-User Operating System 10
sizeof() 134
sorting algorithm
about 65
bubble sort 65, 66
space complexity 66
stack frame 88, 89
static variables 82
storage classes
about 81
global variables 81
local variables 82
program 83, 84
register variables 83
static variables 82
string handling
about 150
declaration and initialization 150
input and output 150
string I/O
about 140
fgets() 141
fputs() 141
structure assignment 106, 107
structure copy 107
structure members
accessing 102
dot operator (.) 102
initializing 102
input and output 103, 104

Structure Padding
  about 105
  verifying 106
structure pointer
  about 111
  defining 111
  need for 112
  program 111
structures
  characteristics 100
  declaring 100
  defining 100
  initializing 102
  syntax 100, 101
  variable, creating 101
switch statement 36, 37
symbolic constants 21, 22

T

tail recursion 91
text files
  about 137
  character I/O 140
  file, reading 142, 143
  file, writing 141, 142
  formatted I/O 141
  reading 140
  string I/O 140
  writing 140
Theta Notation (Θ)
  about 69
  dynamic programming 69, 70
  matrix chain multiplication 70, 71
time complexity 66
Time-Sharing Operating System 8
two-dimensional (2D) array 49-51
type casts 29
type conversions 28
typed pointer 125, 126
types 18-20

U

Union
  about 117
  behavior 118-120
  defining 117
  members, accessing 118
  memory allocation 118
user-defined functions (UDFs)
  about 74
  elements 74
  function call 75
  function declaration 75
  function definition 74

V

valid operations 127
variable
  about 13
  example 14
  rules 14
  syntax 14
variable scope
  about 80
  global scope 80, 81
  local scope 81
void (0)
  versus null pointer 134
Void Pointer
  about 131
  limitation 132
  syntax 132

W

while loop
  about 38
  features 40
  key points 39
  working 39
wild pointer 133